TRANSGENDER UNDERGROUND

glitter books

TRANSGENDER UNDERGROUND
BY CLAUDIA ANDREI
PUBLISHED BY THE GLITTERBOOKS OF LONDON 2002
COPYRIGHT © CLAUDIA ANDREI 2002

AUTHOR'S ACKNOWLEDGEMENTS:

My foremost thanks must go to the staff at Glitter Books, who extended my deadline more than once and who have been extremely patient with me. And, of course, for commissioning this book in the first place.

A very special dankeschön to Jonathan Rigby, who was brave enough to proofread my manuscript without losing his sanity completely. Sincere thanks and hugs to my valued partner in crime, Garo, for sticking with me through difficult times and presenting me with useful literature. Cuddles to my beloved cat Sevig, for being a rascal and distracting me in the nicest possible ways whenever I tried to get extra work done.

Further thanks must also go to Iain at Bryson Printing for technical support and helping me out on numerous occasions with his state-of-the-art equipment (Iain, I owe you more wine than you could ever drink). The same thanks to Tim Warncken for helping me in scanning countless images and making great coffee. A big thank you to Sundjata at Create 24.7 for showing faith in my project and to Alan at Whatsyours.com and other business partners for doing the same.

Special thanks to Pandora De Pledge for providing Andrea's photos. Also, my thanks to Gina Love and Freeda B. – your impeccable taste in so many things proved to be a huge source of visual inspiration. Hugs to my glamboys Preston and Harry for their help. I also would like to express my gratitude to the 'girls' at Ron Storme's and The Way Out Club – without your advice and enthusiasm this book would not have materialised. Last but not least I would like to say thank you to all my friends and models for their endless words of encouragement and their complete support – I know that I'm a bigger drama queen than the lot of you put together!

Finally, have I left anyone out? Sorry. Of course I would like to thank you, too.

NB: Copyright to all photographs belongs to Claudia Andrei, with the following exceptions: Andrea Hillaire's photographs taken by Pandora De'Pledge. Artwork by Claudia Andrei. Leah True's photographs taken by Leah. Artwork by Claudia Andrei.

Cover image: Gina Love; photo and artwork by Claudia Andrei copyright © Claudia Andrei 2002.

About the author:

Multi-media artist Claudia Andrei, originally from Germany, is based in London and works as a freelance illustrator. Claudia studied traditional as well as digital graphics at the London College of Printing. Her work has been exhibited in galleries throughout the UK and Ireland, and her distinctive collage- and photomontage style appeared in music mags such as VOX, The WIRE and MOJO. She has also designed bookjackets for various English publishing houses (most notably Dedalus Ltd. and Serpent's Tail), and is a regular contributor for Shivers Magazine. In addition, Claudia writes for German film magazine MOVIESTAR and for London based paper CREATE 24:7. 'Transgender Underground' is her first major book publication..

WALK ON THE WILD SIDE

Transsexual people are those who identify not so much with their opposite, the male in Jungian terms being complemented by the anima or female component of identity and the female by the animus or masculine counterpart, but rather with a third or recreated sex, and one in which gender orientation is invariably in conflict with biological sex. This state, one of polarisation to an imaginal archetype, which in turn describes its own autonomy can be seen as an act of transformative imagination in which the subject reverses his or her genetic blueprint in the interests of becoming self-created. While gender re-assignment surgery and hormonal therapy together with a programme of psychological adjustment are the necessary medical constituents to completing the process, the real change occurs on a level of psychic healing, and through the subject's attempted integration with a surgically altered body. Of course there's always a distinction between what is imagined, and its approximate translation into physical terms, and the post-op transsexual may feel traumatised by the disparity existing between the two states.

On the contrary the cross dressing transvestite or she-male has no desire to physically change sex. The lyrics to Lou Reed's transgender pop song 'Take A Walk On The Wild Side' give perfect expression to the campness of the transvestite ethos in which a variously gay, hetero or bisexual dominant get their kicks by subverting gender identity. 'Holly came from Miami FLA/ Hitchhiked her ways across the USA/ Plucked her eyebrows along the way/ Shaved her legs then he was a she,' Lou sings, in the monotonal drawl that underwrites his semi-spoken word encomium of the Factory TVs – Holly Woodlawn, Candy Darling and Jackie Curtis. Lou's song not only suspends time by its understated narration, but is a vehicle for the singer to address his obsession with the street cast of Times Square drag queens who were part of his intimate circle for much of the 1970s. Lou's fascination with photographing transgender queens was to extend beyond the level of voyeuristic interest to the relationship he formed with the stunning transvestite Rachel between the years 1974–77, at a time when weird had become his natural expression.

Most transgender people, no matter their categorical distinctions, agree on one thing, and that is the impulse to cross dress and identify visually with the opposite sex starts in early childhood. The artist Francis Bacon was thrown out of home at the age of sixteen by a military father who caught him trying on his mother's underwear. Bacon's early rejection by a disciplinarian father who had little time for an effeminate son with artistic leanings was to have a profound psychological effect on his development as a person. Bacon wore makeup on a daily basis for most of his life, and there's something about the extreme biomorphic distortion of facial planes in his paintings that suggests the idea of radical assault on the norm. Bacon's method of stripping his subject's characteristics to the degree of autopsy could be seen as a prolonged act of revenge on a father who violently disapproved of his son's androgyny.

We can look to history for abundant examples of transgender people occupying roles in the religio-mystical context of their society. In the Golden Ass Apuleius describes the itinerant Galli, who having in their ceremonial worship of the goddess Atargatis or Cybele castrated themselves with a ritual knife, dressed openly as women, and lived by invoking the frenzied dionysian voice of prophecy that came as a direct gift from the goddess. In Rome it was Claudius who adopted the worship of Cybele and the Phrygian rites of self-castration, a cult later replaced by the taurobolium or sacrifice of a bull, as a borrowing from Mithraism. It was the latter ceremony that the notorious cross dressing Roman emperor Heliogabalus (217–221AD) underwent, as a substitute for his own repeated wish to change sex. Heliogabalus who surrounded himself with a court of transvestites, shocked his contemporaries not only by participating in a same-sex marriage with the charioteer Hierocles, but also by his obsession with onobeli, the term used for sailors who were particularly well endowed. Heliogabalus' attempts to undermine male authority in the senate by setting up a rival senaculum, or woman's senate, on the Quirinal Hill, and the innate contempt he expressed for the army were to result in him being butchered in the palace latrines by an outraged splinter-group of soldiers intent on securing the throne for his adopted cousin Alexander.

Also of interest on a historic level are the rites of the Russian Skoptzy sect which survived from the eighteenth century to the outbreak of the Second World War. An unorthodox Christian sect the Skoptzy communes practised self-flagellation and castration as spiritual baptism. Their predominantly gnostic belief in the duality of soul and body being in conflict led them to excise their genitalia in the interests of spiritual rebirth.

Skoptzy castration finds an interface in the Indian *hijras* who persist to this day as a marginalised community in their various incarnations as eunuch, transvestite and intersexual. The word *hijras* meaning neither male nor female, also implies a closed world in which aspects of feminisation are revered for their spiritual and vatic properties.

Most of the contributors to *Transgender Underground* acknowledge David Bowie's ambiguous rock persona Ziggy Stardust as the role model instrumental to helping shape their own feminine realisation of themselves. Nearly all have encountered violence or physical threat as a consequence of cross dressing, but none would wish to revise or be other than who they are. The danger involved in going out transgendered is of course part of the high, as is the need to identify with the exaggerated ideal of the femme fatale through the overuse of makeup. Icons like Marilyn Monroe and Marlene Dietrich remain the glamorous prototypes to which the transgender world aspires. Lipstick will invariably be the hottest vermilion, while the eye makeup will be organised around a palette of sea-blues and greens. The third sex chooses to emphasise its intermediary state by turning heads and demanding attention for what it is – a self-created autonomy. It should be noted that the gay and lesbian community are not necessarily sympathetic to transgender people unless they are of their own orientation, a predicament that further enforces the isolation suffered by those who recreate their gender.

No introduction to a book on transgender ethics would be complete without mentioning Marc Almond's anthemic torch song 'St Judy.' While the song is ostensibly a homage to the gay icon Judy Garland, the sentiments expressed in lines like, 'And if I die before I wake up/ I pray the Lord don't smudge my makeup' somehow epitomise the whole tragicomic narcissism of the drag queen obsessed by appearances even after death. Begun as a minimally arranged acoustic ballad in 1986, the form in which it appears on the *Mother Fist And Her Five Daughters* album, Almond has extended the song in recent years to an epic trip-hop driven finale with which to close his shows, and as a vehicle through which to celebrate not only Judy, but the whole community of sexual outlaws. 'Let's all put on our sequinned dresses/And end it all in tears' he sings, by way of recognition of the irreconcilable paradox at the heart of all those who are made vulnerable by stepping out of gender.

From the seventeenth-century memoirs of the Abbe de Choisy to Proust's serious enquiry into the nature of gender in *A La Recherche*, to Jean

Genet's preoccupation with transvestites as the subject of *Our Lady Of The Flowers*, there exists a rich imaginative literature on what is by nature a fugitive subject. Transgenderism as an imaginative act is what interests me, rather than its existence as a medical or sociological phenomenon. To differentiate and stand apart in one's orientation, be it sexually, creatively or otherwise demands the courage to imagine an opposite, and in the case of the transgender individual to embody it. Wasn't the goddess Athene the brain-child of Zeus, and conceived through the god's head? Transgender people obey a similar archetype, with the transsexual literally giving birth to himself through a similar process of physicalising the anima, while the transvestite is happier to identify with the feminine image he has of himself by recreating it through clothes and makeup. The distinction is of course critical, for although both categories belong to a world of metamorphic variants, one attempts to give physical form to the expression, while the other lives with it as a mental image, and one which is usually disposed of in the workplace.

People largely ridicule in others what they fear in themselves. Transgender people have a hard time on the street, but soon learn the tactics of survival. 'Every angel is terrifying' Rilke tells us in the *Duino Elegies*, and angels we are told are sexless. I like to think of transgender people as intermediaries, and is this the reason why people are frightened in their presence? Rilke said it, 'Every angel is terrifying.'

–Jeremy Reed

INTRODUCTION

Transgender London:

My *Transgender London* project is something I've long had on the backburner, so to speak. It stems from a lifelong fascination with crossdressing. Also, as an artist it goes without saying that I'm intrigued and captivated by the visual and theatrical aspect of transvestism. Yes, there are already a multitude of books and research material dealing with transgender topics on the market. The reader might ask 'Why another book?'. The answer is simple. First, there can never be enough books on any particular theme. Secondly, my book is not so much intended to be a research book, but a first-hand insight into London's transgender community. And this is best achieved by letting its members speak for themselves. It does not necessarily mean that I agree with every viewpoint of those who participated. I merely interviewed my friends, and then compiled and edited what they had to say. This book is not an attempt to come up with scientific research or academic facts. For those interested, there are plenty of such books available.

The reader will notice that those interviewed differ in their opinions about certain transgender-issues just as much as people from the non-transgender community. It is absolutely not a case of 'one for all and all for one' in London's transgender community.

Coming from an illustrating background, I felt it would be the perfect opportunity to capture my models/friends in various poses after their transformation. Hence, the photographs tend to be more on the arty side as opposed to documentary-style. Originally, the project was planned only as an exhibition, but I thought that this would simply not be enough to grab the attention of the public and the media, neither would it do justice to my friends. Looking at photographs is one thing, but reading about people will take the whole affair further. To capture part of their personality by writing about them would be much more exciting then just to capture their persona in a photo. So I decided to write a book along with the planned exhibition, especially after one particular incident happened, to which I shall return later. Also, I have the feeling that crossdressing, which has been around in various cultures for centuries, has not evolved as much as it should have. There is still a big taboo attached to this, and much of modern society as well as the media has no clear idea what being transgendered actually means. With the exception of a few celebrities perhaps, who are upfront about their crossdressing; and certain rock stars (notably Pete Burns) who only make us believe that they are gender-benders by sporting effeminate make-up and the occasional frock, the world of real gender-bending still seems to belong to another galaxy.

Transgenderism is comprised of so many different types that one could fill endless pages. In this book, I decided to concentrate on the following groups: transvestites (TV's), transexuals (TS's), drag queens and androgynes (GT's), or so called gender transient 'in-betweenies'. Furthermore, this book is about male to female crossdressing. Female to male might be another project and another book in the future. Although the non-initiated reader will at first be confused about all the different 'categories', it will become clearer with each page.

A little background information:
Crossdressing in one form or another has existed for centuries. Going back as far as Roman times, emperors frequently dressed up as prostitutes in their orgies. Crossdressing, in a narrower sense, is recorded throughout the Renaissance and in particular in Elizabethan times, during which the part of a woman on stage was performed by a male actor dressed in female attire. Theoretically, these actors would have been the first female impersonators. All this is recorded in ancient manuscripts, but I believe that the history of cross-dressing goes back much further than that, before people were literate. In primitive cultures, medicine-men wore female garments for specific ceremonies, while some native American tribes had the equivalent of our European jester. These non-warriors never took part in hunting and did everything in reverse: from being dressed as a squaw, up to sitting on a horse backwards. In Asian culture, crossdressing is somewhat of a tradition, with theatres and operas performing gender-reversed presentations, like the famous Peking Opera. And not to forget the famous lady-boys of Thailand. The transvestite cabarets of 1920s Berlin and the drag clubs of Paris made history in their own right. But there is simply no such thing as '...just a sweet

transvestite'.

Transvestites are complex people, who aim to transform visually into the opposite sex. Usually, they like to transform as realistically as possible through dress, make-up and female mannerisms. Transvestites are what I would call psychological gender-benders, because they don't have a physical sex-change. Contrary to widespread belief, most Transvestites are not homosexual, although in a psychological context they would have to be bisexual. I believe that belonging to the 'Third Sex' (neither fully male or fully female) is still something which causes not only confusion amongst the public, but also confusion amongst trannies themselves. I noticed that I would often recieve the same answer when I asked them why they feel the need to crossdress. Quite a few replied that they are not sure why they feel this urge. Ohers prefer to hide it from their families altogether and live with a secret, second identity as opposed to coming out. Also, the fear of social ridicule seems ever-present, and I hope that this book will contribute to a better understanding and acceptance of transgenderism.

Transexuals, in contrast to Transvestites, feel the physical need to transform into the opposite sex, because most of them already think like the opposite sex. However, since this physical transition (GRS: Gender Re-Assignment Surgery) is a permanent one, transexuals must prove themselves first by openly living as a woman for one year. Only then will their consultant decide whether they are the right candidate for the operation. Since the consultant's opinion may differ from the opinion of the transexual, many transexuals therefore prefer to go to a private clinic. They would rather pay huge amounts of money than have to wait for their consultant's consent. Transexuals need surgery and hormone therapy in order to treat their condition (Gender Neurodiscord Dysphoria) and achieve physical transformation. Basically, this condition manifests itself when the nerves in the basal structure, which are gender-differentiated in a foetus between the fourth and the seventh month, are either over- or under-masculinized. This happens when the foetus has genetically imperfect characteristics, mainly in androgen reception sensitivity. The problems for the growing child are enormous, because this differentiation of the nerves is independent of the child's genitals. In other words, the child might have a penis and be recognizable as a boy, but he feels like a girl. Likewise, the child might have a vagina and be physically a girl, but she feels like a boy. This condition is very often still referred to as an illness, which it is not. The transexual really is a sexual intermediate, according to pioneering German practitioner Dr. Magnus Hirschfeld. This intermediate condition is triggered when the body produces andrin (male) and gynecin (female) compounds in unequal measures. The glands that regulate these secretions produce too few of either compound, meaning that by puberty or even in childhood the hormonally imbalanced person experiences physical or psychological signs of the opposite sex. For those who experience a gender identity crisis, London has several support groups on offer, like the Beaumont Society (which is a general support group for all transgendered people and their families), or well-known consultant psychologist Dr. Russell Reid.

Drag queens, by comparison, seem to be a breed of their own. To me, the difference between a transvestite and a drag queen seems to be equivalent to the difference between day and night. Drag queens take great pride in dressing 'over the top'. Looking realistic, as far as femininity is concerned, is not always a priority. They are rarely confused about their crossdressing tendencies. I find them witty, brash and of flamboyant personality whilst in drag, but when reversed to the male persona a lot of them are shy and less outgoing. And I have never met a single drag queen who was flattered when mistaken for a tranny. Talk about bitchy queens! I cannot and will not speak for drag queens all over the world, but my drag queen friends seem to dress up not because they feel an urge to do so, but for fun and reasons of vanity. They are just as happy being a male during the week than they are being drag queens at the weekend. People frequently seem to confuse drag queens with female impersonators. In my opinion, being a female impersonator is a profession were the performer dresses more realistic; whilst being a drag queen is a lifestyle and not just a cabaret act. Somehow, the majority of the public always seems to have the stereotypical drag queen image in mind when the issue is transgenderism. Maybe it is because of the images that the media feed us. Drag queens don't always try to pass themselves off as real women, and a man in masquerade is far less intimidating to the average person than a man who genuinely tries to look like a woman.

Androgynes/GT's (gender transients or 'in-betweenies') are not really what could be classified as any of the above mentioned. However, since the classification 'Androgyny' is used for persons who possess characteristics of the opposite sex without necessarily transforming into the opposite sex, I have decided to include some persons from this group in my book as well. One should also make distinctions between those who feel androgynous and those who simply look androgynous. Male androgynes might have naturally feminine facial features, a delicate build or a lack of the usual bodyhair, although this is not always the case. A lot of male androgynes enhance these attributes by applying make-up or wearing feminine hairstyles and the occasional frock, but without going as far as to completely crossdress. Female androgynes might have a very masculine build, small breasts or otherwise less refined features.

But I have always believed that upbringing comes into our gender identity as well. Not in a physical sense of course, but the way we are supposed to behave, think and act is something which is drilled into us from early childhood. I remember when I was a child, my parents always gave me dolls to play with and I had to help Mum in the kitchen (which I loathed). I never really cared for dolls, but preferred to run around in the mud with boys from the neighbourhood instead. And to me it was much more exciting watching and helping Dad making picture frames, than helping my mother to bake a cake. Also, during carnival season in February, I would always dress up in boyish fantasy costumes. I detested all the cute girlie-style dresses and it was not before my adolescence that I acknowledged the importance of frocks....

When I was a teenager, a lot had changed in society, in politics and in music and fashion. Men sporting long hair became as common a sight as women cropping their hair ultra-short. However, a new extreme was reached with the arrival of glamrock. Suddenly, wearing long hair was no longer enough. Bowie and Bolan showed us how amazing a bloke can look in make-up and a frock. Initially, this might not have gone down well with everyone; it certainly went down well with me. Of course, one can't compare glamrock with transvestism. But the glamrock movement made it possible for guys who loved wearing make-up to enter the mainstream. While most girls in my class drooled over the likes of David Cassidy, I was much more taken by androgynous looking rock stars. The more mascara and lipgloss, the better. Featherboas and long gowns? Wonderful! Looking back, this is where my fascination with gender-benders started and it continues to this day.

Putting plans into action:

As I mentioned earlier on, this project was on the backburner for a while. Back in September 2000, the editor of a paper to which I make the occasional contribution asked me whether I would like to write a brief club review. The choice of club would be up to me, as long as the venue was something unusual. So I decided that it might be an original idea to review a transvestite club. I had been to clubs and cabarets before, where drag acts were performed as part of the entertainment. But I never really had been to a club which caters exclusively for trannies and drag queens. I decided that the legendary *Ron Storme's Club* would be a good intro (not that there are that many choices of TV-clubs in London anyway). My friends were either too busy or too intimidated to come along with me, which I found odd. After all, a hardcore fetish club can be slightly more intimidating then a trannie club... or so I thought.

Eventually, a friend of mine, who is the director of a theatre company, was lured into spending a fun night out in a club which would have 'exotic' women galore. Of course, I did not tell him beforehand that these ladies were transvestites. We arrived and I could not wait to get into the venue. I had arranged with the club owner that it would be okay to interview some trannies for my review. Once inside, I turned a little shy and uncertain. Not because we received a frosty welcome, quite the contrary. We received a very warm welcome. I think it was because in previous clubs that I visited, there was always the odd tranny or drag queen. Suddenly I was in a club surrounded by gender-benders, and my friend and I seemed to be the odd ones out. After my friend realized the true nature of these 'exotic' women, he didn't ring me for at least two weeks. I suppose the fact that some drag queens came on to him (to my great amusement) did not make it any better.

Well, there I stood, clinging on to my Bacardi and staring in sheer amazement. Clearly, I was no longer in Kansas! At first, I wasn't quite sure how a real woman would fit into this environment and was relieved to spot a few of my own kind. I was even less sure how to approach some unsuspecting trannies for my interview, in case they felt bothered by my questions. I just felt stupid walking up to them and asking questions along the lines of 'Excuse me please, why do

Liz, author Claudia Andrei, and Joanna Jewels at Ron Storme's nightclub, summer 2001.

you like dressing up as a woman?' Several Bacardis later and I was still no wiser.

Because I desperately needed something for my review, I asked some real women instead. Why do they come to a trannie haunt on a Saturday night? Some answered that they come to the club because their friends or boyfriends are trannies. Others attended because they feel a woman never gets hassled in a TV- or drag club. This was something I had also noticed within the first hour of my visit, and is one of the reasons why I have always felt completely safe and relaxed there ever since. Towards the end of the evening this trannie came up to me and asked with a very friendly smile if 'she' could take my photo for the club website. This is how I met Andrea, who took over *Ron Storme's* clubnight after he passed away, and who introduced me to members of the club who in turn introduced me to their friends. And so I became acquainted with most of my transgendered friends, although some of them I met outside a club environment with a different circle of people. But it still was some way from getting serious about my project.

Making friends amongst the transgender scene:

Originally I was not planning on going back to the club again after I'd had my few answers for the review. But there was something about this whole scene which left a mark on me. I was intrigued and hungry for more, but most of all I was curious. I really wanted to find out what makes these people tick, I wanted to find out about their lives. Of course I went back, and this time I was less shy. Soon after, I became more or less a regular visitor to *Storme's* and also to the *Way Out Club*. I would always hang out there with my new, transgendered friends and chat and dance the night away. I felt proud that I had been accepted into their world. I also came to realize that some of my transgendered friends cannot really be open towards family and colleagues at work, and lead a very isolated life. I hope that one day transgendered people can work and socialise wherever they please, without fear of getting harassed or ridiculed.

Once I got to know my friends well enough and gained their trust, I felt more confident in asking them to take their portraits with the possibility of exhibiting my work. Over the following months, I took endless photographs. A lot of the photo sessions were an absolute laugh. Others were frustrating (at least for me), because some of my models couldn't decide on their outfit for hours on end, and never mind the lips not looking pouty enough. Or they simply threw tantrums for the sake of it. One of the wildest photo sessions took place in Gina and Freeda's apartment (two drag queen friends of mine). It was Good Friday, and the photo session was scheduled for lunchtime. Being the professional that I am, I realized halfway through my journey that there was no film in my camera. Normally this would not be a problem, you simply buy one. But this was Good Friday and most places were shut. Eventually I found a place open, bought a couple of film rolls and rushed over to my friends, already almost two hours late. Because it was Easter, there were lots of chocolate eggs piled up on the living room table and we munched away. For Gina and Freeda, it was just

Model Tamara and I after our photosession in Limehouse Townhall, October 2001.

that. For me it was lunch. After the chocolates we had Campari to drink, followed by another one and another one. By the time the two 'girls' were ready, I was so soused from all the alcohol that I could barely hold the camera steady. In fact, all three of us had problems with gravity, giggling and stumbling all over the place. After we had finished, I left their apartment not exactly steady on my legs. I realized halfway through my journey home that this time around I left my whole camera equipment back in their place! But I must have done something right, because one of the photos from this particular session made it onto the front cover of this book.

Another memorable event occurred during the Christmas season. There I was in the trannie club, exchanging cards and gifts and hugs and kisses, as you do. I did feel slightly unwell that evening, but couldn't think of anything which might have caused it. Anyway, three days before Christmas I discovered to my sheer horror the very visible signs of chickenpox all over my body! Never mind the fact that my whole Christmas and New Year parties were ruined. I spent the whole of the holidays worrying that some of my friends might have contracted it. So I kept ringing round, warning them that there might be a late Christmas 'surprise' in store for them. Luckily, nobody contracted my chickenpox, although one of my tranny friends worried herself into such a state that her skin started to itch. Just imagine: trannies, vanity and the chickenpox. Somehow the combination from Hell.

Life is expensive:

Once I had enough photos to choose from, I decided to put my plan into action and get an exhibition sorted. There was only one minor problem: staging an exhibition with all the trimmings in a proper place costs money. So, the exhibition was on the backburner again and I thought to myself that the sensible thing to do would be to find a sponsor first. I didn't have far to look, because the same editor who originally commissioned me with the club review agreed to back me up and sponsor my project. Most galleries and art venues are usually booked up one year in advance, which suited me. It meant that I had more time to edit my photographs on the computer. Approaching galleries was up to the editor and there seemed plenty of time.

One incident too many:

Meanwhile, I continued socialising with my transgendered friends. It was during one Saturday evening that the incident occurred which I mentioned earlier and which made me realize just how ignorant and abusive members of the public can be. A tranny friend of mine gave me a lift in the car, down to the club. We arrived a little too early, so we decided to stay in the car for a while and chat. The car was parked on a street next to the club and this group of youngsters (of the tracksuit and baseball cap variety), who were all sitting on a stone wall nearby, seemed to stare at us in a way which alarmed me. Eventually, one of the guys walked over, looked in the car and noticed that the woman behind the steering wheel was not really a woman at all. He called his friends, and they all came over and started to shout abuse at my friend for being a tranny and they also shouted at me for sitting in the same car with 'this freak'.

At first we tried to keep our cool and ignore it, but things took an even nastier turn when one of them started to kick against my friend's car. It really pissed me off, and I stuck up my middle finger in complete disgust. This was the moment when my friend decided it might be a good idea to drive off, especially since one of the lads picked up an iron bar from a building site close by and headed straight for the windscreen. Luckily, we escaped in time with only some scratches on the car. We both were visibly shaken and it made me realize that it's not all glitter in the world of transvestism. Needless to say, we did not make another attempt to park in the area. On a separate occasion, I witnessed a tranny being attacked by a bunch of hooligans on the way to a venue. They smashed a bottle over her head and the poor soul had to seek shelter and ask for help from the bouncers, blood dripping from her forehead. There were several other events, such as somebody observing a tranny getting out from her car, and when she got back the car was all demolished and the stereo stolen. Of course, this happens all over London to all sorts of people. But on this occasion it happened because the driver was a transvestite. That's when I decided that staging an exhibition would never be enough. I wanted to publish my experiences and those of my friends in book form. And, indeed, I finally found a publisher ballsy enough to publish a book about ladies with balls.

There is a first time for everything....
In my case, getting the book together, as well as the exhibition, proved a much more difficult task than I thought it would. For starters, it meant spending almost the same amount of time interviewing my friends as it took taking the photos. All this got even more complicated when my father fell seriously ill. I had to go back and forth to Germany and support my family. I also went through a personal crisis and very often did not feel inspired to carry on. The whole project seemed to drag on (no pun intended). Eventually, the situation did become slightly better again, and when I was informed that my sponsor had got me a venue for my planned exhibition, I decided to work extra hard. After all, I owed this much to my transgendered friends.

Choosing the appropiate style of writing (monologue) was, as a matter of fact,

Harry and I freezing in Chalk Farm, March 2002.

the easiest part. I had to be extra careful not to disclose any information which may cause embarrassment to my friends. That is the reason why during the interviews for this book most used only their transgender name. In addition, my transvestite and drag queen friends in particular, would only pose for me after they put on wig and make-up in order to conceal their true identity. As their friend and photographer I naturally know them as they are in daily life. But drag and transvestism is about illusion, and I did not want to strip off this illusion unless my friends wanted me to. Such precautions were not necessary for my transexual and androgynous models. The way they look in my photographs is the way they look in real life.

Before I close, I would like to add that, despite the occasional frustrations, putting this project together was an experience I will never forget. It has introduced me to some truly amazing and colourful people and I sincerely hope they won't be disappointed with my efforts. Finally, I hope that all was not in vain. By that I don't mean that I expect to get rich from this (I won't). But if this book could contribute to a deeper awareness concerning transgender issues, it would fill me with pride.

–Claudia Andrei, London, March 2002

Author Claudia Andrei with Gina Love, London, January 2001.

GINA LOVE

"Hello there, I am Gina Love, drag queen extraordinaire and originally from Birmingham. But I live and work in London, as it's a lot easier to dress up and go out. I think one experiences a little prejudice in the rest of the UK. My age? Hasn't anyone ever told you that it's rude to ask a lady about her age, darling? Only kidding. I am 37 years old, but I felt transgendered from childhood on without any confusion, although obviously I did not crossdress back then.

"When I'm all dressed up and look at myself in the mirror, at what I have achieved, I feel much more confident and stronger from within. I also feel that looking and feeling like a woman gives me a better and far more sensual choice of clothes. However, due to my carreer (which, very conveniently, is a fashion designer) and hectic lifestyle I dress only at weekends, when I can relax and enjoy the experience fully. But I do go anywhere when dressed in drag and on the whole I get positive reactions. I certainly have wonderful experiences every Saturday night! Only sometimes I get hassled, but nothing really bad ever happens. In fact, it was my humble self who inflicted bad experiences, because initially I drank too much when stepping out in drag. Believe it or not, I really thought that drinking a lot and dancing too much would boost my confidence. And wondered what went wrong, when ending up with a face like a swamp and feet like a sponge cake!

"One really bad experience due to excessive boozing was on a vodka- and cocaine-fuelled night out. I discovered this ghastly gash on my foot halfway through the night, deep red and black and totally disgusting; like something out of a David Cronenberg movie. Anyway, I became more conscious of, and paranoid about, the gash as the night went on, but because I was so high I seemed unable to do anything about it there and then. I was sure the wound needed hospital treatment and I would not live to see the next morning due to blood-poisoning. Later on (actually it must have been about 5.30am), I was sitting in this café on Old Compton Street, completely out of it. A friend of mine insisted that at least she should clean the wound, and with help from staff she arrived with antiseptic and bandages. After she took off my high-heeled shoe, she proceeded to clean the wound. Only to find out the gash was nothing more than a squashed chunk of chargrilled kebab with tomato, stuck onto my skin! Needless to say, my friends didn't think the experience was a bad one; they still were in hysterics weeks after the incident.

"These days, I have the confidence to step out in drag and, yes, being a drag queen has filled my life with glamour and escapism. But like many women, I myself have mood swings and from time to time I feel I can't be bothered dressing up. Once my mood swings are over, I have to escape from the daily chores and routine by being very glamorous again. And I enjoy nothing more than looking glamorous and being a sex goddess. Anyway, most of my friends are transgender or drag queens as well, which makes it easier for me. My partner is also transgender and we both evolved at the same time. So from that point of view it makes the daily drudgery much more bearable. Even my mother was fine with it (and the fact that I am gay), and my dad and my sister also know what I do, although we don't usually talk about it. As for my workplace, I keep my personal life separate. For the simple reason that my employees wouldn't really understand why a man would want to dress up as a woman.

"To me, transforming means a lot more than just dressing up: I have had a few procedures done to my face to make it look more feminine, but I have to be careful not to cross the line. Or else I could run the risk of looking freaky in day-to-day life. On a couple of occasions I tried laser treatment on the face, but decided not to carry on with it because I like to look like a man during the week (stubble etc). As for hormones, at this present time I wouldn't consider taking them. However, to some people it doesn't seem to make any difference whether I look like a real woman or like a man in drag, as the following incident, which happened to me in New York, demonstrates. My friends and I were on another wild night out, this time in New York, but relatively sober. We just stepped out from the infamous *Vault Club,* in full drag of course, and got into a cab. After a while I noticed that we were being followed by this large vehicle to our left. I became conscious of this because the vehicle pulled up whenever our cab stopped (next to traffic lights etc). So I couldn't help but pout and tease, hoping for a hot night of lust. I finally decided to make eye contact and was horrified that the prospective shag turned out to be a Rabbi dressed in full regalia – gliding his tongue across his lips and wanking himself off. Just how did you guess that after this discovery I didn't bother making any further eye contact! This really was the topper of the whole evening, although I had a pretty bizarre experience even inside the *Vault Club*. There are different playrooms and levels to this club, and in one, which seemed to cater for the more exhibitionistic S/M clientel, I spotted this drag queen lying on a rack – legs wide open and her arse exposed for everyones viewing pleasure. At first I didn't really see that she was pushing this massive dildo in and out of her rear end, and when she waved at me to join her, I simply walked over. When I realized what went on, it was a little too late to make my exit. She asked me to push the dildo for her, but I was far too bewildered by this sight and politely declined the offer. However, I did not want to appear totally rude and ignorant, so I made conversation instead. Yes, we were talking make-up tricks and the latest fashion, while she kept herself busy with this damn dildo. Just an average night out in NYC, I guess.

"I hope that sharing a little of my life has given you at least some insight into the camp and adventurous world of a drag queen. Or maybe it's just *my* world which is camp and adventurous. The world could be even more interesting if people in the UK wouldn't look down so much on crossdressers. A bigger awareness would be good, but there will always be a stigma associated with crossdressing. I feel that in Europe people have a much more liberated attitude on the subject. As for Gina Love: I guess one day I'll be buried in those heels, so that says it all."

TAMARA / MATT

"I am a 19-year-old drag queen and call myself Tamara. I was born in London but have only lived here a year and a half; before that I lived in Cambridge. Living in London it's been easier to venture out alone, or in public places. I think this is largely due to the fact that Cambridge is such a small place and that I knew too many people to go to places other than nightclubs. But apart from that there is no real difference. Only that there is more on offer for transgendered people. Mind you, to me it has never been a case of feeling transgendered, but more putting on the clothes and realising that they work with me.

"To me the most exciting part of feeling female is... all of it. It is not a sexual thing, and I certainly don't get off on it. But with the character I take on, I'm much more forward. I do things in drag that I wouldn't even dream of doing if I wasn't dressed up. For a start my wardrobe contains mostly girls' clothes. Doing drag as both a hobby and for work does affect your life in a very big way. My friends love it and encourage it. If it wasn't for my friends I don't think that I would do it so much. It's something that has provided many hours of amusement for both myself and them.

"Also, drag has been my workplace and still is. For a very long time people told me that I should do it as a job and not just for fun, so after a while I eventually did. I had long hair for three years which I despised, but because I did drag I couldn't really cut it off. (I have now.) It also affects the way you view your body. Whereas the average male would like to have a toned and slightly muscular physique, I cannot. It simply looks too masculine in drag.

"As far as dressing up is concerned, for me it's mainly a weekend thing due to the fact that this is when I am working. But if there is an event during the week I don't mind making an effort. It doesn't bother me when I do it, as long as I look good. Equally I don't have a problem with going to most places in drag, just so long as I am safe. The reaction of people when I go out in drag is definitely more positive than negative. But then I have never really cared for people who don't like it. If they have a problem it is for them to deal with, not me. I am proud and

totally at ease with myself as I know my direction. I don't in any way feel confused about my gender and who I am.

"When I socialise, nine times out of ten I am the odd one out, but my drag girlfriends Aaliyah and Saskia have been known to come out on occasion. I would say that I enjoy all of it. Every time I socialise in drag something new and exciting happens, so it's all good. Fashion, music, clubs – there is not really anything that I do out of drag that I wouldn't do in it.

"The only bad experience I've had was when a cab driver tried to sleep with me. I came home late one night from a party in Chelsea and took a cab. Throughout the the whole journey home, the driver was very suggestive and flirty with me, obviously not realizing I was a man. Perhaps I should add that whenever I'm in drag, I speak with a high-pitched voice. I didn't know quite what to do, so I told him I was working as a receptionist (as opposed to a professional drag queen) and was engaged. To emphasize my lie, I showed him a diamond ring on my finger. Of course, this didn't stop him from making further advances towards me. In fact, his hands were all over me and he then said that I wouldn't have to pay him for the fare. Instead we should go off and have some fun. Unfortunately his idea of fun was not my idea of fun, so I repeated 'I'm engaged!' but to no avail. He continued to fondle me and insisted we should have some fun. Although there was a certain amount of flattery involved in his persistency, I decided that enough is enough. So I tuned back to my normal male voice and said 'Look mate, I've got a cock' – and you can guess what his reaction was. Funnily enough, he still offered to not let me pay for my ride, only this time to get me out of the cab as quick as possible!

"This experience had two sides to it: apart from the unpleasant aftertaste, it made me realize that somehow I must look extremely convincing as a woman. As I said before, until recently I had naturally long hair and when I was dressed as a male, people often mistook me for a female even then. Never mind the fact that I had no make-up on and was wearing clothes that were obviously male. So for that reason I don't think anything changed. I'm not on any form of hormones or undertaking any kind of sex change treatment. It is not something that I think I would do, as I am happy with the person I am and that includes my gender. I know where I'm coming from and where I'm going to and I know my

sexual orientation – not everybody is so certain about it. For example, I think that most crossdressers display a gay attitude because they are unsure how to act. There is a big difference between a real woman and a man in a dress. Men tend to go over the top and go really camp, as this is traditionally how crossdressers have acted. For example, cabaret-drag queens and pantomime dames have traditionally been the only time a lot of people would have seen a man in a dress.

"I'm not sure about the future, that is something you will have to wait and find out. I am at an age where a few decisions about my aim in life must be made. And one of those will include being a drag queen. It is something that I would like to continue, but in what capacity I'm not sure. After all, this is not just about my beliefs and attitude, but also about how others perceive me and transgendered people in general. There should be a bigger awareness of crossdressers, and the only way to do that would be to see and hear about it in everyday life. We have openly gay actors, film stars, music icons and politicians. Why not out-of-the-closet crossdressers? After all, you never can tell. I think the attitude towards transgendered people or crossdressers is one of ignorance, whereas being gay and homosexual is something that people are used to. It is seen much more often in the media, crossdressing is not. We do have crossdressers in the media, but not that many in this country. The only two that the average household would know about are Lily Savage and Dame Edna."

KIRSTY

"I am Kirsty, a bisexual, 35-year-old pre-op TS. However, by the time this book goes into print I will most likely no longer be pre-op. Originally I am from Dulwich, London. I started to feel transgendered from early childhood on. I have always known that I was TS, so it is my life! Couldn't imagine being any other way. My family are not happy about the situation, but still communicate with me, although they do keep their distance. The few close friends I have were shocked to find out about me, but are still close friends. I think that both family as well as non-transgendered friends are shocked about the lengths I go to in order to achieve my final transformation. I am on hormones, blockers, and laser treatment at the moment. If I get the finances together, I will also consider facial reconstruction, boob enlargement, SRS...anything goes!

"With work it was a different story: when they found out, they offered me a girl suit for work straight away.... Applause and admiration was the response at my work Xmas party, to be honest, I was shocked by their response! With regards to my partner I have to say that I could never have a relationship without them knowing about me first. My partner is transgendered, too.

"When I step out as a girl, the reactions I get are always more positive... never had a bad reaction yet. There is this pub in Woolwich and me and Sandra went there one evening, all dressed up. We got a bit pissed, and I overheard this conversation between two real girls. One was saying to the other: 'If you take your jeans off, I'll buy you a drink.' So I walked up to one of these girls and said 'If you take your jeans off, I'll take my frock off' and she goes 'Never, you wouldn't do it anyway.' 'Oh yes, I would,' I replied. This time around, she seemed to believe me, and suddenly all these excuses came up regarding her underwear looking second rate. But I did take my frock off and still looked smashing with my basque and stockings on!

"I tend to socialise anywhere. At weekends my friends are nearly all TG, but at work when we go to the pub, I'm usually the only transgendered person. I feel the urge to transform into a woman most of the time, and the admiration and

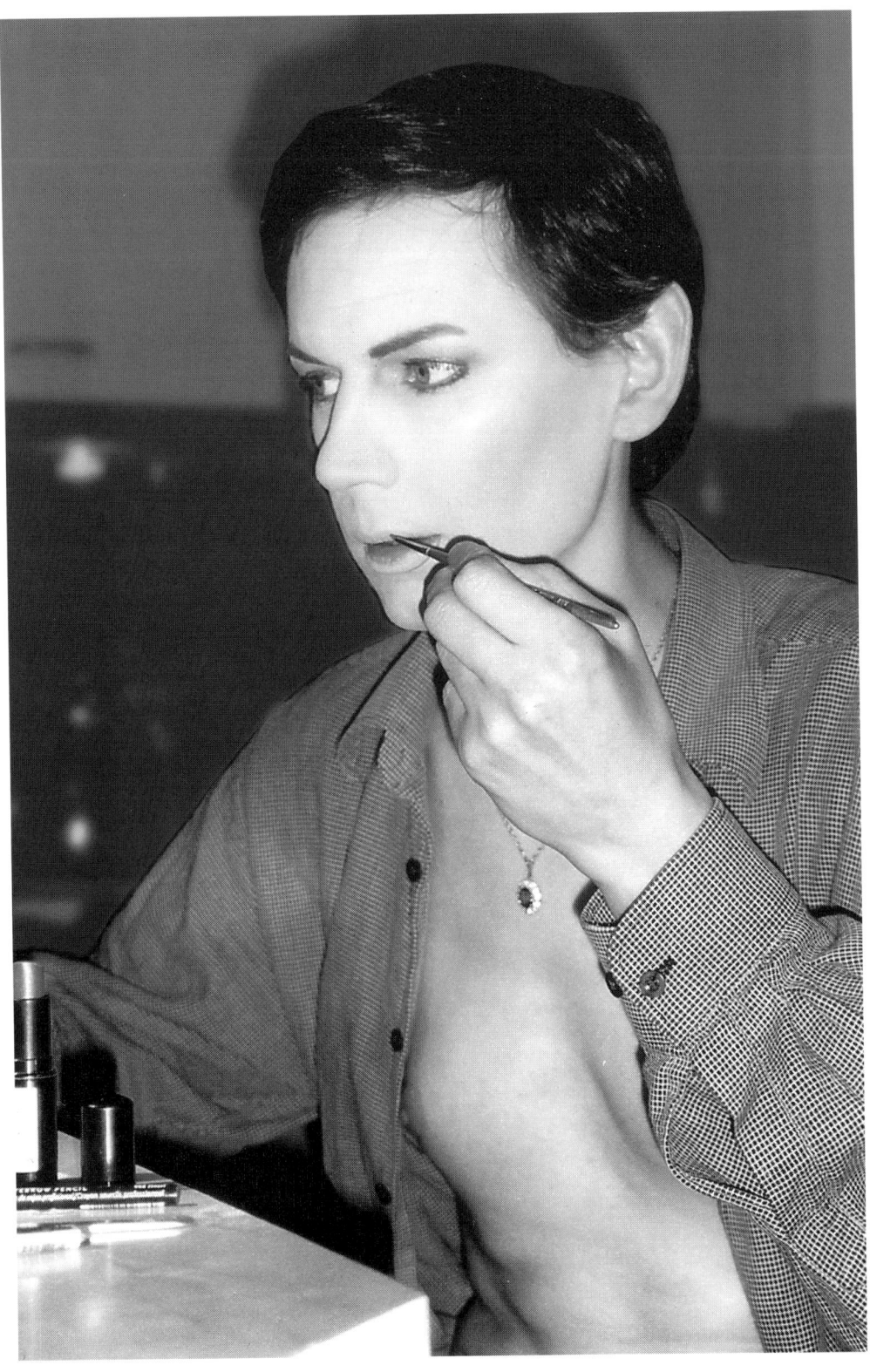

attention I get excites me. I have met so-called straighties when they first came out, but once they are overcome by their inner effeminates, they would go out with a gay or even like to be seduced by one! I have never had any particularely bad experiences as a TS. In fact, I've had many good experiences, but nothing stands out. On second thought, there are some rather amusing anecdotes which I remember.

"After an entertaining evening at *'Ted's Place'*, which is a well-known trannie haunt, we were making our way back to the car. We, that is my friend Sandra and myself, for your information. Anyway, a passing motorist, with obviously impeccable taste, leaned out of his car window, eyed us up and down, 'wolf whistled' and shouted 'oi oi'. Unfortunately, whilst doing this he failed to notice the taxi that had stopped ahead of him picking up a fare... There followed a crunch, hooting of horns and an exchange of colourful language. 'It's nice to be noticed,' said Sandra. 'Abso-blinkin-lutely,' I replied!

"On another night out, police pulled me up for doing 60mph in a 30mph zone. Their car was on the side of ours, and when they got out of the car and approached us, the policemen realized that there was something 'funny' about us girls. Anyway, when the first policeman saw that we were two trannies, it was surely something his training had not prepared him for. So he just put up three fingers, said '30mph' and both coppers drove off, utterly unnerved.

"When asked whether there should be a bigger awareness towards transgender issues, my reply would be that I'm not so sure whether there should be one. I think the attitude of the public towards crossdressers etc. is mixed if they have never met one, but normally positive if they do. As far as I see myself, I can only say that I am proud to be transgendered and, hopefully, in the future I will be working and socialising permanently as a woman. At the moment, when I am in boy-mode, my spare-time activities are cabinet making, gardening and music. When I am Kirsty, my hobbies are shopping, make-up and music. Who knows what my spare-time activities will be when I am Kirsty full-time?"

SANDRA

"My name is Sandra, I am a forty-something TV from the UK, although I prefer not to tell the exact place I am from. I feel that for me as a TV, staying in London is more tolerant in certain areas, but worse in others. I started crossdressing when I was six years old and went to primary school. I felt this way until I was sixteen and then I lost interest due to a huge influx in hormones, I believe.

"When I was twenty, I got married and had a son. After about three years of marriage I realized that I had done the wrong thing and the marriage broke up a few years later. When my wife asked me whether I had another woman, I answered "Yes, I am the other woman.' She couldn't really take it on board at all. So we split and I took a flat in Hastings, where I worked as a hostess for the Beaumont Society, which is a self-help and support group for transgendered people and their family and friends.

"My parents do not share my enthusiasm: they have disowned me. But my son is okay about me being a bisexual TV. And there where other girls who said to me 'Don't go to places like *Ron Storme's* or *The Way Out Club*, cos they have a sleazy reputation. So of course I went there at the next opportunity. I didn't find it sleazy at all and enjoyed myself immensely. Also, I met my transgendered partner Kirsty there, and we are still together today. After I met Kirsty, we and my son all went to *Ron's* for a good night out. Mara, another transvestite, came on to my son big time, and that was the beginning of a wonderful friendship between Mara and me.

"I usually only get a chance to go out as Sandra at the weekend, because work dictates. I feel much more liberated as Sandra, I love the admiration I get when I'm her. I socialise anywhere, but also enjoy dressing up in private. The reactions from others are on the positive side, but of course, you do get the occasional bigot. My circle of friends consists of other 'girls' really, and we all hang out together. I am not aware that my personality changes when I am transformed, I will only say that some crossdressers may display a more gay attitude when dressed as a girl.

"Being transgendered was a little confusing for me at first, but I'm now content. I feel confident when I transform into Sandra, but I probably would feel even more confident if I could afford liposuction. I also tried hormones, but it turned out not to be very practical due to my size (6'5" tall). So for now, I am literally just being me. Not that I feel less confident all that often, because I don't get to go out all that often. I simply do not get a lot of spare-time due to work. If I do, it is usually spent on clubbing. Because of my lack of free time, I cannot recall any bad experience as a TV, nor any really good experience.

"But I can recall a funny one, which happened a while ago: there we were all dressed up and looking forward to a jolly night out. So off we go, out to the car. Kirsty goes to put the key in the car door, fumbles and whoops, she drops the keys straight down the drain grid... Now what? Fortunately, I had a set of house keys. So I go back indoors, lose the wig, put on an old anorak and jeans (over my mini and cami top), find a magnet and some string and went fishing for keys! Time passes. I finally manage to retrieve the keys up from the depth of the sewer. Passers by. They might have wondered why some big guy with make-up, wearing an anorak and jeans with high heel shoes on, should be lying down on the pavement with his arm down a drain hole....?

Eventually, I got cleaned up and we finally drove off, only about an hour later than planned. NOTHING will stop a tranny from having her night out!!

"On another night out, this time in the *Philbeach Hotel,* we spotted someone famous from *The Rocky Horror Picture Show.* At first we were a bit surprised to find this person in a trannie hangout, but on second thoughts it wasn't really that surprising. Anyway, I thought that I was being recognised by him (this was the real surprise), and that's how we got into conversation. So *Rocky Horror* person tells us in confidence that a certain actor from *Baywatch* came up to him once and begged him to play *Frank N Furter.* Both Kirsty and I roared with laughter when we imagined this scenario. As far as I can remember, this was about the only time we really laughed during our chit-a-chat with *Rocky Horror* person. To be honest, he wasn't the best conversationalist, so we made our excuses and hit the bar.

"So there you are, this is my story. Or my story within my story. I don't have much of an idea what the future holds for me – please get me a crystal ball. I don't have much of an idea what the attitude of the public towards us will be in the future either. But I think and hope it will be more tolerant as time goes by. Most of all, I think a more accurate image of us should be conveyed."

PRESTON H.

"My name is Preston H. I am 24 years old – but 17 forever. I consider myself to be an androgynous being, though not human but an alien. I come from the stars, planet Swan5 to be exact. On Swan5 we are pure light and energy. But I re-emerged in human form in the Holy Land of milk and honey – IsraHell! In order to live on this planet, I had to take on the shape of the mortal boy that I am now. But I think that I am something more advanced than female and male earthlings. Not sexually, but in the way of my thinking. I know it's hard to understand and it's even harder for me to explain, but I believe that the people who do understand this do so with their heart and the depths of their mind. I'm here to try to change the world. It is humanity's last chance to redeem itself. So me and other likeminded beings are trying our best to help with this redemption.

"Even in human form I do feel like an alien. My persona started as the frontman of a band called *Strangewise*. Preston H. Bizarre was my alter ego, just like Ziggy Stardust was Bowie's alter ego. I went through crazy times – being in the army during the week wearing uniforms, the lot, and then going to the band's gigs and to clubs as Preston H. After a TV programme was made featuring myself as Preston H, I became known as this character. I suffered from a split personality of some kind for some time. But now I am whole and one. I found myself after long searching. I still have to find the place around me. So, being an androgynous alien is my persona most of the time. It's also a metaphor for being different. We all feel alien sometimes – I just hope there are enough boys who feel like kissing and loving the alien.

"I divide my time between IsraHell and London, because of several club projects I'm involved in. But more about that later. I feel like the ugly duckling, but whenever I come to London I understand that I'm a swan and there are other swans around me. Although I am considered different even in London, and that is part of the fun. I'm not sure whether you could describe me as simply effeminate, I am more than a boy or a girl by being neither of them. As I said, I am more this androgynous alien, but being a gay glam-boy is my chosen human form. Gay all the way! I don't think that one's sexual orientation has anything to do with the way one looks. I was aware of my orientation from the human age of 13 onwards, when I was attracted to other earthling boys and, well, other beautiful creatures.... Planetary and inter-planetary creatures.

"I would not consider taking hormones or having laser treatment, no. I believe in nature. The only thing I do is work on my muscle-tone. I want to look in the mirror and see something I like. I have the privilege to be attracted to myself, because I'm attracted to guys. And my mirror image reflects someone good looking... Shouldn't we all be something that we consider attractive? The gay community in IsraHell especially seems to have a problem with being effeminate: they think if you like boys then you should look like one. It does not leave me with a lot of choice while I'm in my native country. I used to look more androgynous in the past, but unfortunately had to find out that gay boys don't seem to like it that much. But here in London it is much more relaxed, although my androgynous looks are more part of being glam, and not so much being a woman. Anyway, I feel different from human beings, I want to create a fantasy.

"Creating a certain fantasy is also what my clubs are all about. They are my way to change something in this world and to touch and alter people's lives. I want to create the places that as a unique person I would go to but which sadly don't exist. And so I have an international production company called *Pose Productions*. We have a club for gay and transgendered people in IsraHell, we have *Glam-Ou-Rama* in London and we hope to get another club started in the USA as well. *Glam-Ou-Rama* is the best club in London for years, the comeback of gay glam and glitter and a real fun place for gender-benders. Glam has always been related to that, and we want to offer a venue especially for the younger generation of androgynous beings, and those who feel young forever. Of course, *Glam-Ou-Rama* (info: www.glam-ou-rama.co.uk) is for everyone who can appreciate style and originality. You even get extra credit for being eccentric, flamboyant and a wild dandy. Anything goes in our clubs, especially as far as sexuality is concerned. Girls, boys, she-males, aliens and whatever else in between. There is only one rule: freedom über alles! People sometimes underestimate the power of small changes, but it's like a small stone being thrown into a sea which creates big waves. You never know what will happen. We are open to anything.

"But not everyone is. I feel that by and large transgenderism is still misunderstood. Society should treat TGs as being something normal and not treat them like freaks. Being transgendered or being gay or being whatever should be something natural. In my country we have Dana International, who is like a symbol. No one cares any longer that she was Yaron Cohen before the sex change. But had she not won the Eurovision Song Contest and became the international star that she is now, perhaps people's perception of her would have been less tolerant. Obviously she felt that she is much happier and sexier as Dana than as Yaron, but how many people can relate to that?

"As yet I have not completely given up hope with this planet, but if humanity continues its course of self-destruction and intolerance, I shall retire back to planet Swan5 and observe all the madness from a distance. My advice to aspiring aliens in the meantime? GOD GAVE YOU MAKE-UP, USE IT WISELY!"

SASKIA

"I call myself Saskia. I am originally from Venice. The best way to describe me would be a transvestite-drag queen. I am happy that I can express this side of me since I moved to London, because there is no real transgender scene in Venice. There are some transexuals, but they are mainly prostitutes. Over here, I can express my transgendered side more openly and safely. Altogether, it has turned me into a more open person. Also, London has special places to go, although I tend to socialise everywhere. I have felt 'different' since I was an adolescent. What I mean by this is that I took an interest in crossdressing and transgender issues. But, as I have already said, I did not openly express this side of me until I moved to London. I am thirty years old now, and I feel that things are pretty good for me as a transgendered person.

"I am neither a weekend nor a full-time crossdresser. I'd say fifty-fifty is more the case. After transforming, I get a real kick out of the way I look and all the attention that I get. But, in terms of my character, I stay the same person. The same can also be said about my physical appearance. I feel that I could do with a nose job, chin refinement, bigger lips and boobs etc. However, I don't think I would really go ahead with plastic surgery. This is because I'm not sure whether I would ever want to be a full-time 'girl'. I might consider laser treatment and some hormones in the future, but right now I don't want to change my life.

"What I mean when I say 'I don't what to change my life right now' is that I don't want to reveal the fact that I crossdress to either my family or my colleagues. I have a very well-paid, creative job and do not want to risk losing it. On the other hand, my girlfriend knows that I crossdress. Not only is she relieved that I came out, but she really likes my 'other side'. As for my circle of friends, I will say that I've lost some old ones since I came out, but I gained a lot of new ones – mainly here in London.

When I step out in drag, I step out with a circle of friends comprised of both transgendered and non-transgendered persons. Wherever I turn up dressed as a girl, I usually get very positive reactions, in equal measures, from both men and women. Occasionally, I do get slightly confused reactions. For example, one incident which happened during the London Mardi Gras left me slightly bewildered. I asked my friend to take a picture of me with a police officer, just for fun. We spotted a police officer along the road. I asked him if it was alright to take a photo of him and me together. 'Sure', he replied generously. After the photo was taken, I asked him whether he would mind posing for another one, this time with me hugging him. 'I wouldn't do it if I was you', he said sharply, and then walked away. To this day I don't understand why my second request freaked him out so much. Perhaps it has something to do with the fact that people are rather ignorant in general. Maybe they don't know what to say and how to react when they see a tranny.

"Another incident, also involving the police, clearly demonstrates what I mean. The first time I went to the *Philbeach Hotel* (a social meeting point for TVs, TSs and so forth), I had a conversation with a 'girl'. She/he told me that he is a very famous tutor at the University of London. After a pleasant evening, he offered me a lift home. Before that, however, he changed his clothes in a very discreet manner. He did this to ensure that people would not recognize him as we walked out of the *Philbeach*. While we were driving to my place, we were stopped by police for a routine check-up. They asked the tutor to step out of the car and very soon realized who he was. A short while later, I was asked to step out of the car as well. When they realized that I was a tranny the policemen looked at each other. It became clear that they did not know how to react. I'm certain that they were thinking something steamy was going on between this famous tutor and myself! I'm not sure what the policemen thought.

"It might be the case that people have a notion of transgendered folk being generally gay even though a lot of us are not. Or it might be the case that some crossdressers display a more gay attitude once they are dressed as a girl. Whether I display a more gay attitude when I'm dressed up is something I'm not aware of. I admit that I like teasing, but I would not do anything to hurt my girlfriend's feelings.

To be honest, it's about time that the media did something in order to bring a greater awareness of transgender issues to the public. The media have a lot more influence than we do. Also, we 'girls' should start to come out more in public and not just hang out in places where trannies socialise. I am very proud to be transgender, and the way I see myself now is the way I will most likely see myself in the future."

PURPLE PAUL

"Purple, that's definitely me! I love the colour purple. Most of my clothes, make-up and even part of my furniture are purple. Hence my name Purple Paul. I am 35 years old and originally from Maidenhead, Berks. My father is English and my mother is from Bermuda.

"I think the terms 'transvestite' or 'crossdresser' don't really apply to me. With me, it's more the case that I naturally look like a girl. I think that other people find my behaviour more feminine, but it is not conscious on my part. For me, living in London is certainly safer, not just because of my feminine looks, but also because of my partly ethnic origin.

"As I already said, I don't consider myself typically transgender, although I was mistaken for a girl even during my school years. It might have made my life easier if my Mum had admitted me to a mixed school, because I always got a lot of abuse from all the other boys at school. As a result, school does not hold fond memories for me....

"I socialize everywhere that would be considered safe (scene-like) and I go to any place I feel like going. I am more into dressing up in a feminine kind of way, because when I'm dressed in a more masculine way people still accuse me of looking like a girl. So why restrict yourself to one set of clothing when women's clothes tend to fit me better anyway, especially sarong-style dresses. There is simply more choice for women. I pick bits and pieces from everywhere, as long as it is comfy. My big influence in dressing is my Mum, she is a very well-dressed woman. Everything always matches perfectly. Also, when I was a teenager, the fashion then was the New Romantics. This fashion movement was very accepting of androgyny, so I jumped right in. In addition, I love wearing some make-up to enhance my feminine features. I always make sure that my naturally nice-looking fingernails are perfectly manicured and varnished, preferably in all shades of purple and lilac... However, my most treasured asset is my hair. It is good hair and happens to look extremely feminine. This is particularly handy as I am a freelance hairstylist. From that point of view, my looks (or should I say my locks) never were an obstacle for me at work. My other profession is being a musician, so my androgynous appearance works for me, not against me.

"I would never consider plastic surgery, laser treatment or taking hormones. I just make the best of what I was born with. People behave strangely enough towards me as it is, because of my feminine looks and because they don't know what to make of me. Can you imagine what their reactions would be if I'd look even more like a girl? My family never really had any problems with my appearance. In any case, I reckon that they had more problems with me being gay than with the way I look. Having said that, I remember one incident years ago when I was in my Mum's kitchen with a friend. At that time I didn't sport naturally long and curly hair as I do now, so I decided on these really long hair extensions until my own hair would grow to that length. Anyway, when my Mum came home from work, she could see my friend and some girl in the kitchen, but not me. Imagine her surprise and shock when I turned around, and the 'girl' turned out to be her son! I don't think she was very amused...

"My circle of friends consists of all types: men, women, gays, straights and in-betweenies. When I go out with friends, I never feel like the odd one out. I am not odd, but very proud to be myself. Also, I never switch from boy-mode to girl-mode and back, I am just myself all the time. This includes both female and male characteristics. The reactions I get from strangers are both positive and negative. Positive in terms of getting complimented on my looks, negative in terms of verbal abuse (also because of my looks). One time I was even chased and verbally abused. This happened one Saturday evening on my way to a party. I was in an off-licence getting ice when I noticed this bunch of Caribbean men had noticed me. For fairness' sake I must admit that I was made up in a truly stunning manner that evening. And also because I fit into that pale-black female stereotype that most black men have of black women, I got noticed even more. When I left the shop, they shouted 'Batty Man' after me, referring to the fact that I looked queer to them. I tried to ignore it and walk away, but they followed me. Eventually one of the guys confronted me, so I tried to escape by saying 'And if I am, so what?' and I walked around him. Then he tried to hit me. That's when I decided doing a runner would be a good idea! I ran into a police station close by, but before that the guy tried to hit me with a full water bottle. Luckily, he missed.

Leah True

Leah True

Leah True

Joanna Jewels

Joanna Jewels

Harry

Harry

Preston H. Bizarre

Preston H. Bizarre

Andrea Hillaire

Ronessa

Elizabeth

Elizabeth

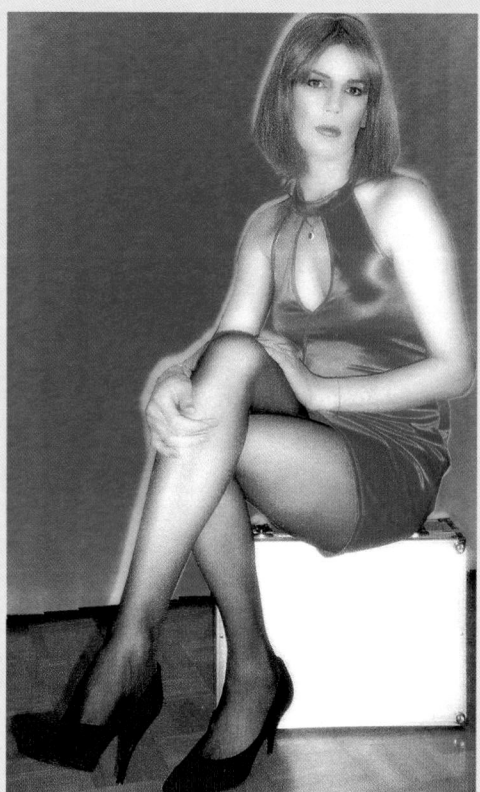

Kirsty

Kirsty

Kirsty

Sandra

Sandra

Purple Paul   **Purple Paul**

Saskia   **Saskia**

Wilfreeda Beehive

Wilfreeda Beehive

Gina Love

Gina Love

Wilfreeda Beehive

Tamara

Tamara

Lisa

Mr. Charleston

Mr. Charleston

Alan

"Crossdressing and the attitude of the general public... that's a difficult one. I think the general attitude towards crossdressing can best be described as fearful curiosity. I think there ought to be a greater awareness towards transgender issues, but how this could be achieved is something I'm not so sure about. Maybe through transgendered soap characters? After all, soaps seem to influence the public like nothing else."

JOANNA JEWELS

"I am Joanna Jewels and I consider myself to be a transvestite. It means that my gender identity is combined of both male and female characteristics at the same time. This has been my condition since adolescence.

"I am originally from South Africa, but since arriving in the UK, I have lived mainly in the Home Counties. In my case, I would feel more confident about living in London as a transvestite than where I live now. Like most large cities, London has its fair share of diversity and eccentricity. I feel I would fit in better there than I would in more rural towns. After all, easy-going folk in rural places are perhaps not so used to seeing the unusual. If I were to live in London, though, I would definitely consider becoming a woman for most of the time.

"When I'm dressed as a woman I feel so well and at ease with myself that I don't want to change again. When I discard everything masculine about me and put on feminine externals, I become completely calm. To me, it is such a step forward to see myself in the mirror as a woman, all the femininity and the clothes on my body overwhelm me. To crossdress as a woman for most of the time is something I've always wanted to do. Unfortunately, I am faced with the impossibility of this every day because of where I live and the job I'm in. Therefore, the only time I get to become a woman is at weekends, which is never enough for me. Sometimes, the desire to become a woman is so strong that I tend to go for a walk late at night, all dressed up. I realize that I put myself in danger by doing so, but I make an effort in my appearance as much as I can. I only walk the streets when I feel confident enough that I look convincing and inconspicuous. But the fact remains that whenever it becomes possible, I will give up men's clothing.

"Now that I'm more confident and happier as a transvestite and I tend to spend more time in my female role, I think it has certainly affected my life. It seems that my feminine nature has taken control of my masculinity, and everything a woman wants, I want the same. I'm definitely becoming more dependent on money now than I ever was. Without the financial means I wouldn't be able to support the lifestyle I now lead, so I have an extra job to earn more. I'm also more conscious about my health and beauty. I keep in shape and stick to a daily regime of cleansing and moisturizing my skin. Part of my job used to involve manual labour, but I'm not so keen on that any more either. Anything that involves heavy lifting, I generally don't participate in. This has already had an effect on my job, but now I'm the company salesman and it's not so bad any more. My job hasn't been affected by me being transgender. As one of the sons in a family firm, I have some advantages, and that is that I will never get laid off or given the sack. Generally, I get treated well by fellow work colleagues. I try and keep my transgender life as private as possible at work and never really talk about it to anyone. Not that it would cause a real problem, as most of them already know. But it's not worth adding more fuel to a fire that's already lit.

"Although I have never talked about my crossdressing tendencies to any member of my family, they have always had a suspicion about it. I felt that this started around the time I left school and began college. I recall seeing an article in a Sunday supplement magazine about mothers and their sons who liked to crossdress – this was the first time I saw boys dressed as girls, and I became totally excited about it. Shortly after, I went to London and bought my first dress, which I tried on in the toilets and on my way home. I wore my boy clothes over the dress so I wouldn't be carrying any suspicious packages when I got home. It seemed a little strange to my family that I'd been out in London all day and had nothing to show for it, but I think that secretly they knew what I had done. Prior to this I used to wear mostly my mother's clothes, so they might have been out of place in the wardrobe most of the time. She also found my woman's underwear and stockings in the laundry, as I had them mixed up with my other clothes. There weren't any girls in the family and so I feel there was enough evidence of what I was doing. Despite all this, my relationship with my family hasn't been affected that much by what I do. We may have had the odd argument and fallen out with each other a few times, but which family doesn't.

"With my friends it is not really a problem, as my current friends are either gay or transgendered and as I tend to socialise mainly in TV-clubs anyway. There was a time when I hung out with a mostly 'straight' crowd; this was during the days when I was very confused about myself. I think my friends back then suspected that I might be gay, although I am not, because I never seemed interested in women. I just hung out with this guy all the time who happened to be my best friend. I was attracted to him in some way, not sexually, but just that he seemed very sincere and kind. There weren't a lot of guys I knew who were like that. I felt I could talk to him about anything, and I did. About my dressing up for example, which in those days I tried to keep very secret. Eventually he met this girl and also had to move away with his parents, so subsequently we didn't see each other any more. Eventually, we lost contact. As with my other friends from my early days, we slowly all went our separate ways, and as for me, the fun hadn't even started...

"With regard to my partner, I never really had a long-term female partner to come out to. It seems somewhat difficult to find a girlfriend when one feels like a girl most of the time oneself. And since I'm not gay, I'm not really swinging the other way either, at least not sexually. With the experience I've had up until now, I can only say that the majority of gay men, including the more effeminate ones, find transvestism thoroughly unpleasant . They really wonder why a man would want to wear a dress and be like a woman. I've visited numerous gay clubs and bars and have hardly met any transvestite. However, some gay men do perform as drag queens, but they see that as a part of their culture and it's all for show. But I feel that it has nothing to do with transgenderism. It's not unusual, though, for transvestites to have had a homosexual episode. But this is by no means inborn; most that do this would usually enjoy both sexes and have therefore a bisexual urge.

"I was confused about feeling transgendered for a long while. At first, my male being was absolutely not in agreement with my feminine tendency, and it was a tough battle until I accepted the fact that I'm a mixture of both sexes. I am very proud of being transgendered now, and I think that most of our kind feel the same. Why should we be ashamed of ourselves? I think we should have equal rights and if ever there is total freedom everywhere, many women would be better fighters than effeminate men, who do their duty in other ways. The reactions I get when dressed as a woman are mixed, some people can be very accommodating about it, yet some others find it hard to accept. Occasionally I've been able to show myself in broad daylight, which is the hardest test for any transvestite. Sometimes men complimented me on my looks, women would just give me a smile or look anxious. But here and there it did happen that I was discovered as being a man, despite all my efforts. I still have a masculine appearance and I am over six feet tall. I haven't had many bad experiences when dressed. There's only one incident that sticks out in my mind as particularly bad. It was when I was fairly new to the scene and I had just met this other trannie at one of the clubs I frequented. 'She' invited me back to the hotel where she was staying for coffee and a chat. When it was time for both of us to call it a night, I left the hotel realizing that I forgot my car keys in the hotel restaurant. What's worse, I was now locked out of the hotel and wearing only a short dress in the freezing cold. By now my new friend had probably gone to her room, so there was no getting back in. I couldn't just stand there and wait until the hotel re-opened again in the morning. I had no choice but to ring the doorbell endlessly until somebody heard it. Eventually a girl came to the rescue and let me in, but just when I thought I can get my keys back I realised that the hotel restaurant was also locked! I managed, however, to track down the room number of my new-found friend, and stayed with her until the morning. Thankfully, though, I have no other stupid incident to report.

"I used to believe that in the future, my peculiar talent would fade away with increasing age or stop altogether, but the opposite is the case. My tendency towards transgenderism is greater than ever and I will certainly pursue my drives in the future. I will try and perfect my feminine side as far as my physical appearance goes, but I don't ever see myself completely transitioning. At the moment I am not taking any hormones or other substances to increase my femininity, but I might consider it at a later stage, especially herbal hormones which are not so strong. As a transvestite, I would love to have softer skin and softer hair, so from that point of view it is very tempting. With regard to laser treatment, I would certainly have that done. I think every man would love the idea of never having to shave again. Cosmetic surgery is one thing that I have done in order to make my facial features look more refined. I'll probably end up paying off my debts for years to come. But hey, it was worth every cut. It might affect some of my spare-time activities such as painting, photography and shopping, as these are costly hobbies. Still, I don't regret what I have done in the slightest.

"My final thoughts on transgenderism? The public perception of us is very poor. Most people think we make a choice to dress up as women, when really it is an inborn condition. To us it feels natural to behave like a woman. We also tend to falsely be considered homosexual. Whenever I tell people of my condition, usually their first question is 'Are you gay?' The media could do a lot to bring the right message across to people, but very often manages to portray us in the wrong light. Maybe the education board could teach children about transgenderism in school, along with sex education. But whether this will happen in my lifetime, well, I doubt it."

RONESSA

"My name is Ronessa and I am a transexual, originally from Malaysia. I live in London because, as a transexual, it gives me more freedom and choices of places to go. It also allows me to gain more acceptance at my workplace due to the 'Human Rights Act 1998', as well as the equal opportunities policy employers have to abide by. Anyway, most of my colleagues have accepted and respected my choosen gender role unquestioningly. And my managers have been extremely supportive and understanding.

"I already felt transgendered from childhood on. When I came home from school, I used to put on my mother's clothes and wore my mother's make-up. By the way, my mother knew this and was very tolerant towards it, as she thought this was part of my growing up phase. She often encouraged me to wear female clothes, because she really wanted a girl after having three sons. So basically, I was the daughter she always wanted but never had. By large, my family have always been very supportive and understanding, although I did have problems with my dad initially. He told my mother off for being so tolerant towards my dressing habits – he was certain it would turn me into some sissy. My true friends have always loved me and accepted me for the person I am and not my gender identity. Being a transexual has never really affected my partner either, because I've always been more feminine then some biological woman. I enjoy being a 'girl' more than some real woman. To me the most exciting aspect of feeling female is being able to be treated like a lady and taken out by my boyfriend. And naturally, being able to dress up and feeling confident is an added plus, especially when I'm admired by men and women. I also enjoy the opportunity to wear my hair long, paint my nails, etc.

"I don't consider myself as a weekend nor a full-time crossdresser, because I don't crossdress as such. I have always felt like a woman, think like one, act like one and look like one. Therefore I am now a full-time woman. I would not consider plastic surgery in order to make myself look more feminine. I am very happy with my natural looks which I've been blessed with. God was very kind to me when he created me (guess he must have taken extra time during my creation). The only help I have is hormone treatment, but no laser treatment. Because I am of Malaysian origin, I have naturally very soft and smooth skin all over, with very little hair growth.

" Being transgender has made me feel more at peace with how I've always felt, and not having to supress my true feelings. I am no longer confused about what I am. I am proud of what I am because I always try to live like a woman. The only time I was ever confused was when I tried to live like a man due to family pressure once upon a time. But now I am in the clear about my identity, and my feminine look emphasizes this. As far as my sexual orentation is concerned, I felt like a 'straight' woman all my life. Of course, sexual orientations vary completely as far as other transgendered persons are concerned. I can only speak for myself, but I do think that a lot of crossdressers may masquerade their outside look. By doing so, they are not going to change how they feel inside, regardless of whether they are dressed up as a girl or not. Perhaps they feel sexually less inhibited when they are dressed up as a girl.

"I don't socialize exclusively in TV or drag clubs, I socialize wherever I feel like going. And the reactions I get from others are defintely more positive. I get a lot of compliments frequently, especially from men, but from women as well. However, I try not to get too big-headed about it and keep my feet firmly on the ground. What is inside my heart is more important than my looks. Reactions I get from others, i.e., the general public, serve as feedback on how I present myself and what they think of me. I think I've passed as a woman 100% and nobody (apart from my friends) knows I am a TS. Unfortunately, a good few transgendered people are under the illusion that they look feminine simply by sporting wigs, make-up and dresses, when it is obvious that it is a man. This does not exactly contribute to a more tolerant approach from the general public towards crossdressing, especially transexuals. At its best, the majority of people will end up looking at transgendered people simply as 'drag queens', an image most have implanted already. And because of this, the majority of the public will not be able to see beyond this stereotype, and not be able to acknowledge the various types of the transgendered community. There ought to be a bigger awareness towards transgender issues. One has to lead by showing a good attitude and example in order to achieve greater acceptance from the public. There should be more media coverage on the subject, e.g.

differences between TV, TS and so forth.

"Personally, I never had any bad experiences as a transexual. Apart from perhaps being hustled by men who tried to get off with me, even though I made it clear that I wasn't interested. The good experiences have been meeting the love of my life and making a lot of friends, both like myself and non-trans friends. When I go out, I mix with all types of people and feel very positive about it. I am me and they are what they are. I do not discriminate. My spare time activities are those of a woman, not of a man. I don't engage in masculine activities. Shopping for make-up, buying feminine clothes, shoes, doing photographic modelling, house- keeping, cooking, sewing etc. are the things I enjoy doing in my sparetime. As you can see, these are clearly non-masculine characteristics and activities. I am a very feminine TS, I am a 'female' female. With regards to the future, I see myself no differently to any other man or woman. I have fully accepted my gender role without regrets or mixed feelings. I know what I want in my life."

ALAN

"My name is Alan. I am 34 years old and I consider myself to be a transgender. Originally, I am from Scotland but I have lived in London for years now. In fact, it was by coming here that I started to realize who I was.

"I have felt transgendered since my childhood, but whatever inborn identity I had, it was always suppressed by society. I tried not to let my gender affect me in a negative way, and as an adult person I was strong enough to come out to family and friends. Now I feel blessed by the fact that I know who I am.

"To me, feeling transgendered is as natural as eating or breathing so I don't consider it to be an act of transformation. I do not go out and try to pass as a woman. I also don't have the urge to change my whole identity but simply like to enhance some of my features. Because of this, I would draw the line with certain treatments – for example, I would not consider taking hormones. For me, it's a bit like going into Dr. Jekyll & Mr. Hyde's medicine cabinet.... One thing I would quite like is getting rid of my facial and body hair.

"As for my family, they got a real shock when I came out but ignored it thereafter. Now that I live in London, it's out of sight and out of mind. With my friends it has never been that much of a problem, although one of my best friends felt a little betrayed (why couldn't I confide in her earlier?). My male friends are quite sensitive people and had no problems with it anyway. Being open is the key.

"Fortunately, there was never a question of coming out to my girlfriend, as I was my feminine self when we first met. That was when the most incredible thing happened – she did not notice or, rather, she did not take note. At the party where we met, there was another guy, physically rather similar to me but a more masculine, leather-clad type. When I disappeared to get the drinks she panicked, as she did not know which of us was me! Some people find this hard to believe, but those who were there know it's true. So do we, which is most important.

"My workplace is no longer a problem either, but getting to this stage did require a couple of changes. For starters, I left a successful media career to start my own business. This worked fine, but, as I have discovered, it was not really what I wanted to do. Ever since I got a taste of the fetish scene, its tolerance and its people, I wanted to put something back into it. Similarly, as I talked to my 'normal' friends, I realized they too missed a safe, non-threatening environment to explore their sexuality. Hence, www.whatsyours.com, an on-line magazine aimed as a bridge between the so-called mainstream and the broadly understood alternative world. It carries the message that it's okay to be different and that there is nothing wrong with kinks and alternative lifestyles. We must be doing something right, as we have just won an Erotic Award for the Website of the Year 2001.

"To be honest, it took years to become confident about being transgendered and get absolutely clear about my sexual orientation. When I first came out, I wondered if I was gay. I thought I had to fancy men because I also have a feminine side. The outside influence played a big part in it, as a lot of people think that as a transgendered person you've got to be gay (they can't distinguish between sexuality and gender). At least for me, this is not the case.

"I believe that each and every one of us is made up of both feminine and masculine elements, and what identifies us is a peculiar mixture of both. For me, being transgender is about accepting and understanding one's feminine side, rather than trying to suppress it. It's treating the masculine and the feminine aspects as complimentary elements rather than hostile oppositions, thinking in terms of 'as well as...' rather then 'either/or'.

"The way I see myself in the future is positive. People usually remember me and want to remember me; they are more interested in my personality than in what I wear. I want to have a family one day and will bring up my kids in the spirit of truth and tolerance and tell them who I am when they are old enough to understand. I hope this will teach them that people come in all shapes and colours and, for that matter, genders and sexual orientations. What's yours?"

LEAH TRUE

"I am Leah True, a 37-year-old transvestite from the UK. There is not really a TV scene where I live, but in London there is a much greater variety of clubs, bars etc., with people who are more open-minded and tolerant. I feel comfortable knowing that I will not be recognised, as a man, that is. When transformed into a woman, I love to be recognised, but obviously on a positive level. A negative reaction would upset me as it would be a blow to my self-confidence, and make me realise that my feminine look was not as convincing as I had thought. But no matter how convincing, the illusion crumbles as soon as you open your mouth, because that's the giveaway and people realize you're a bloke. It can be dangerous, because if a man who, five minutes earlier fancied you as a woman, finds out you are male, then his sexual ego can be shattered. He can turn nasty and violent indeed. Still, for me it is simply a sexual turn-on to pass as an attractive woman, to the extent that men will often attempt to chat me up without realizing my true gender. I remember on one occasion, whilst fully dressed up, coming home from a shopping trip in Newcastle, a man hurried by me. On rounding the corner of the deserted underpass, he stopped and exposed himself to me! I gave him a disdainful look of 'Is that it?', and continued walking on. It's debatable who would have had the bigger surprise, had I returned the compliment!

"On another occasion, my girlfriend and I went to see Limahl (of Eighties band Kajagoogoo) play at a reunion gig in the Roadhouse, and I noticed him staring at me from the stage several times. And a couple of other guys from the audience tried to chat me up also. Ironically, nobody attempted to make a pass at my girlfriend, and she is pretty hot-looking by any standards! After the gig we were invited backstage, because I know a member of Limahl's band. Anyway, Limahl kept looking at me and finally came over to introduce himself to me. I said 'My pleasure', and at that stage he realized that I'm a man. I got a little nervous at what his reaction might be, but he just smiled and commented, 'Nice tits, mate.' Obviously a pop star with great taste and a sense of humour...

"Generally speaking, I do feel sexier as a woman than as a man. Unfortunately,

the dressing-up bit is usually restricted to the weekends going to bars and clubs, both straight and TG. Dressing up and buying clothes for the first time is a sexual turn-on. The favourite season for any trannie is Xmas, because a transvestite can walk into a department store and revel in lingerie, pretending it's for the girlfriend... If I would feel more confident being a woman during the daytime and in public, my crossdressing activities would not be restricted so much. I am working on it, though. And one big boost was when recently I won the title of 'Alternative Miss London' in the *Way Out Club*.

" I have laser hair removal. I would consider talking hormones as well, but it's not likely that I'll take them due to worries about side effects. The other thing I would consider is facial surgery, mainly a nose job and tracheal shave, which is the removal of the 'Adam's Apple'. But I'm not sure when and if I will proceed with the surgery bit.

"Before 'coming out' as a transgendered person, which I realized from childhood on, I felt isolated, and felt that any relationship would be in jeopardy as it would involve 'living a lie'. I now feel my life is complete and I have made many friends and admirers. Of course, the best thing which happened to me was meeting my girlfriend. And contrary to popular belief, many TVs are hetero, I certainly am. Some of us may like the attention of men as it heightens our feminine persona, but are not necessarily turned on by this attention in a sexual way. My girlfriend and I met while I was dressed up, and the result is our love for one another! As for my family, they don't know of my TG activities, and I don't want them to know about it. People at my workplace are not aware of my 'other side' either. But I certainly have no lack of friends, quite the contrary, I now have three different circles of friends: 1) Old friends who do not know about my transgender activities, but I feel that I am drifting away from them, as I can't be open when discussing my activities in London. 2) New friends I've made in the transgender community, amongst them very special people who understand me on a much deeper, personal level and share a common bond. 3) Other non-transgendered friends in London, who are totally accepting and we all are comfortable with each other.

"In short, I am a happy transvestite over all, and I am proud of the level of feminity I have achieved so far, and the friends I have made. I am not too

worried about something bad happening to me as a crossdresser, because all this time nothing bad has happened to me ever. I would go so far as to say that the attitude of the general public towards us is mainly tolerant, depending on where you live. I even hold the opinion that there need not be a bigger awareness towards transgender issues. One of my future ambitions is growing old disgracefully and having enough time to pursue my interests. Which include cars, photography and cinema when I am in boy-mode, and photography, sex, shopping, sex, socialising and more sex when I am Leah. Being Leah is exciting!"

ELIZABETH

"I am a 42-year-old hetero transvestite from Norfolk who crossdresses occasionally. Normally I attend TV events only, although the occasional shopping trip has been known. Whenever I'm in boy mode, I shop for 'her'. The female dressing first started as a young boy (approx. eight years old) and continued in phases until I reached my early thirties, when the need to dress en femme occured on a more regular basis. This culminated in my first visit to a London TV venue when I was 37.

"My social outings are now to TV or fetish clubs, which presents an opportunity to experiment with different dress styles, colours and hair styles. When I go out, many of my friends are also transgender. I have never had any really bad experience while wearing women's clothes, but those people who notice will sometimes laugh and point you out to others. One just has to ignore them.

"On a lighter note, crossdressing can lead to unexpected experiences with the public, and very funny ones at that. Once I was sitting in a room with ten other crossdressers, when an electrician walked into the room and asked where the broken down TV was. He then appeared to be very confused and bewildered when everybody fell off their chairs with laughter. I kid you not. Or when the company I was working for adopted a positive discrimination policy to promote women into senior management. A colleague suggested if I wanted a promotion I should start to wear a dress – if only he knew! Or did he anyway ?

"Family and colleagues are not aware of the crossdressing aspect of my life. Certainly family members would find it difficult to understand, a situation familiar to many in the transgender community. My non-transgendered friends also don't know about me crossdressing. I must admit that being transgendered confused me at first, but now I am okay about it. My social life seems more relaxed and I enjoy meeting people who have similar experiences, problems, interests and outlook on life.

"Unlike several other transgendered persons I met/meet, I feel equally comfortable as both Elizabeth and as my male persona. I like myself when I am a man, and I also like myself when I am 'her'. I would not change anything about my appearance. For starters, the bone structure of my male body can't be changed anyway: hips, shoulders and jaw are as they are and that's it. Perhaps I will consider laser treatment at a later stage, we shall see.

"But laser treatment or not, it still won't change the attitude most of the public have towards crossdressers like me. They don't want to understand and see us as strange people. To the general public crossdressing is seen as something to laugh at. There is very little understanding of the subject or acceptance for those concerned. Television shows and press articles often sensationalise the subject and try to portray crossdressing as some kind of strange, freakish activity.

"However, TG issues appear to be slowly receiving a more balanced press coverage as the Church, police and military now accept transgendered members of staff. There was a time when lesbian and gay relationships also had a similar press coverage but, with the advent of characters appearing in soap operas, these members of society are no longer perceived as unacceptable as neighbours, work colleagues or members of family.

"Even other types of television shows occasionally include couples in relationships from the same sex – mainly shows depicting the couples buying property or re-decorating neighbours' houses. This all helps to portray a life of normality for this type of relationship. They still have to live on a budget or have slight differences of opinion, with a compromise found just as any other heterosexual couple would work it out. Young and old are watching these programmes, and it all helps to create in the public mind a feeling of acceptance and so helps to remove the shock factor.

"For example, a male to female TS character is portrayed by a female actress in *Coronation Street,* but a transvestite has yet to have the equivalent positive image transmitted into living rooms three times a week. If this did happen, maybe the taboo of crossdressing would be reduced and become more acceptable. The character then would be seen by the general public as no different to others, who dress in their sparetime as Cavaliers and Roundheads re-enacting battles of the Civil War!"

ANDREA / ANDY

"My name is Andrea Hillaire, I come from London and, sorry, I can't tell you my age, haha. Since I spend quite a bit of time as 'Andrea', I guess I must be an in-between. My nails are long and painted and very soon I shall no longer be wearing a wig. Also, with eye make-up on most of the time, I think I am closer to being a transgender. I prefer not to tell you my sexual orientation, as it would destroy the mystique surrounding me.

"I think that I have always felt transgendered, working in very high testosterone areas dressing as a woman never really stood a chance. I started dressing very late in life, mainly because I had done most of the things that I wanted to do. Only the urge to dress like a woman was unfulfilled. I just love feeling female. Being Andrea is a side of my personality which had always stayed hidden. As Andrea I become extremely confident, outgoing and achieve far more in just about everything I tackle. People seem to like Andrea a lot more than my male side, and who does not want to be liked...? I don't really transform into a woman, my female side simply has emerged and I feel extremely comfortable with it that way.

"I have become very well known throughout the transgender community as the girl who takes thousands of pictures. My website, which I started when I first started dressing, is jokingly known by some friends as the HELLO Magazine of the transgender world. I am now hostess of *Stormes,* one of London's most popular and successful nightclubs. I have been on television twice so far, once in a television drama (as an extra) and on a television chat- show as a special guest. There are some more television and media things being arranged at the moment. My social calendar is quite hectic with invitations to all sorts of transgender, gay and media functions. Most importantly of all, I have made hundreds of wonderful friends, like Susanne who instigated my coming out as a transgender. Without her support I think it would have been years before I attempted it. Others? My friend Linda has been there for me from day one, I still bounce anything I do off her. Pandora De Pledge is largely responsible for the way I look today, and my friends Leah and Sue are the source of so much fun and friendship. Becoming transgender has transformed my life and opened up so many new opportunities for me, without which I would be leading a very boring existence. What few friends that I had as a male have not deserted me, in fact they have all been brilliant. Since I had so few friends as a male, most of my friends are transgendered. The strange thing is that as time goes by, I seem to be making more friends as Andrea. Perhaps I am more communicative and easier to talk to in my feminine guise. I do go out with male friends, but as Andrea, I am more comfortable in that guise.

"My family have not really been effected that I am aware of: My parents have the opinion that as long as I am happy then that is the most important thing. My brothers and sisters are all okay with my lifestyle. Everyone at work is also absolutely brilliant, they accept my feminine ways and there is no nastiness at all. I am really lucky or should I say Andrea is. A couple of girlfriends were a bit angry with me at first, but they are still my girlfriends and they seem to have accepted what I do. Well, it is not as if I have become something horrible. I have no problem travelling around the UK as Andrea for various functions, and also to be with friends for a night out anywhere. I definitely notice the positive comments I get. Compliments do wonders for my ego despite being a naturally humble person. Negative remarks, what few of them there are, tend to go past me unnoticed.

"I am extemely proud to be transgender, proudly going about my business with a completely clear conscience. After all, I am doing nothing wrong. If a woman can walk around in socks, trainers, pair of trousers and a shirt, why can't I walk around in tights, bra, panties and a dress? Have you noticed that a lot of ladies' lingerie manufacturers now have a range of women's pants that look like men's? I am taking herbal hormones to help me develop boobs and I also do chest exercises. I would not consider chemical hormones because of the health risks. I don't need laser treatment, I do not really grow much facial hair. I use a product which retards hair growth and is said to mimic balding naturally, it seems to be working. I have not shaved my face for over a year, so I am using the product to lessen the hair on my arms now, which are not really that hairy anyway. I would like a nose job, I think my nose is too masculine. There is not much else I would change, unless they can shrink hands (since mine are a bit large).

"The majority of people I have met seem to be very friendly towards me, despite the fact that I am a man in women's clothing. Therefore, I can only really comment from a personal point of view on what the attitude of the public is. I consider myself lucky to be so well received. But most certainly there should be more awareness of transgender issues; the general public have so many misconceptions about us. The transgender community is pretty much like a 'normal' community, we just wear the clothes of the opposite sex. There are gay, bisexual and heterosexual people, but no-one questions this if you are wearing the clothes of your own sex. The majority of the media needs to stop treating the transgender community as something seedy, sexually orientated and an object of ridicule. Most of the time for a transgender person to be of use to the media, it has to be for a sexual nature. Perhaps it is time we had a transgender newsreader or chat-show hostess instead of another comedian dressed as a woman for laughs! Hopefully in the years to come I shall have more than one club to be hostess of, a sort of transgender Stringfellow. You never know, if I am lucky enough I might even get the chance to be that transgender chat-show hostess. Life is very short, I have lived half of mine being too serious and I intend to live what is left having fun doing the things I really want to do."

LISA

"My name is Lisa and I am a 29-year-old transexual, originally from Liverpool. Living in London makes everything a lot easier for me, because here the people are a lot more like-minded and open-minded. I felt transgendered from early childhood on. Even at highschool I had a feminine hairstyle and wore make-up, even though I was officially still a boy and dressed like one.

"For me, feeling female is natural and I never really felt any other way. At first it made my life more difficult, because in the past I was ashamed about the way I felt. Also, I had to face a lot of prejudice at school and beyond. But for exactly the same reason, my life now is more fulfilled because I am proud to be transgender and no longer confused.

"Since I've transitioned, I've got new friends. What makes me particularly proud are the TG-people I have met. Okay, I lost a few old friends, but gained many new ones, so it was a profit. My family have been nothing but wonderful and have really supported me; the same can be said for work. I work in an almost entirely female environment and my colleagues knew me pre-transition, and not much has changed now.

"I remember a rather amusing incident at work: I met a colleague for the first time since I transitioned into a female. Before that, I had only worked with her while I was still a man. She noticed I had the same surname, but didn't realize I was the same person she had worked with before. She asked me if we were related or if I was Steve's wife (Steve was my name when I was a male). I answered no and then she proceeded to tell me how she hadn't really enjoyed working with Steve, and that I (Lisa) was much nicer.

"The reactions I get from others are mainly positive. I don't have a regular partner, but the men I do date are great about it. I consider myself completely hetero, but I would say that crossdressing can change some aspects of sexuality temporarily. As a transexual I am now a woman all the time and I do not crossdress.

"In the future I see myself as living the same life as any other woman. Right now, my whole life is a good experience. The only bad experience I ever had regarding shifting my gender was with my GP, because in plain and simple terms he was a pig!

"Right now I am on hormones and anti-androgens. I had laser-treatment in the past, but I don't need it any more now. It's been about a year now since I've been on hormones and I will continue to do so until my operation; after that I will have to take a lower dose. I've had facial surgery already (jaw and skin contoured) and this will be followed by my final GRS (Gender-Re-assignment Surgery).

"When I go out to socialise, I go to all sorts of places. A lot of my friends are transgender, and a lot aren't. Those who are not don't make me feel that I am any different from them. One of my favourite spare-time activities is singing. I've been performing regularly for the past six months at various venues in London. My own music is mainly R&B. Also, I won a starsearch with my version of Madonna's 'Hanky Panky'. However, the final is coming up soon, so we shall see...

"I am not so sure how serious I am about my singing career. On one hand it would be wonderful if I have some success with it. There is certainly the opportunity to exploit the fact that I am a transexual, and hopefully a talented one. You never now, the music business might have a field day with it, haha! And I am not so sure how the public would react to such news either, it could range from very positive to very negative.

"I do believe that TS-men/women who are role models and make a success of their lives will certainly contribute to a more tolerant understanding coming from the general public. Chances are that the public is more open-minded towards it than the record companies, they just love to play so safe these days. But I am taking singing lessons, and if I could gain some success, of course I would be thrilled. Right now it is my other job which pays the bills and I also enjoy it, so it's not as if I'm absolutely desperate. However, I am positive and open about the future and it will be interesting to see what it holds for me."

HARRY

"I am Harry and I'm not TV, TS or inbetween. In some ways I do feel out of place in this book project because I'm not a crossdresser. But in other ways I fit in perfectly, because I'm androgynous and effeminate and love wearing make-up, just like a TV or TS. Superficially speaking, I fit into the same mould by living a similar lifestyle and also understanding this kind of life – not that any two people have the same life!

"About three years ago, back in Glasgow, my story was quite a different one. I didn't dress up and hardly wore any make-up back then. But that was because I didn't really ever occur to me to do so. Looking back, I think I always felt different, I just didn't know how to express myself before I moved to London. Glasgow seems so medieval. You just don't get people like me there; at least you never see them. The few times I've been back there, I get insults and confused looks everywhere I go. Not just in 'bad' areas of the town. People there simply don't know how to react, and that includes my family and friends. A man in make-up? Never!

"In contrast to Glasgow, my life in London has been an eye-opener from day one. When I moved here I went out a lot more than I had in Glasgow. There are more clubs here and a much wider style as well. Musically I was after glam/indie clubs where Bowie was King. (Or should that be Queen?). This took me to Madame JoJo's where I first encountered transvestites. I just went for the music and enjoyed meeting people. I didn't think about it as a transgender issue, it was just a club playing music I liked, with people in it I could relate to. It didn't matter if they were dressed plainly or done up in drag. Going there changed my attitude to appearance, and now over 3 years later (I'm 28) I'm a lot more confident in how I present myself. People might look at me and ignorantly think I'm gay – I'm not. But I know that as long as I'm in a busy part of town or stay somewhere accepting like Camden, I get much less hassle. In fact, I even get some appreciation.

"Even in Glasgow I did sometimes wear a little eyeliner, but now I am more comfortable with wearing far more make-up. Not that I feel the desire to look like a woman; I never feel female. But I think that it makes me look better and emphasizes my androgyny. At one stage I considered laser treatment for the hairs on my shoulder and chest. But it doesn't bother me enough to consider it seriously, I can always shave. Women are the fairer sex. They dress up, put on some paint and look even better. I only have a man's body to work with, but I try not to let that stop me looking good. Sometimes I dress up more extreme, put on a wig and look like a girl. But it's just an attempt to look good, not to transform. I'm vain, not female! I can't even go to the corner shop without fixing my hair, making sure my make-up is perfect and being happy with my appearance. When I'm made up, I do feel more refined, more elegant and more attractive – though many people, of course, see it otherwise.

"Sadly, my parents belong to those people. They don't really understand me. I try to explain that in my case it's mainly vanity, but they don't get it and are afraid. Because what you don't understand you are frightened of. The idea of me taking part in this book project embarrasses them. This saddens me. I can only hope if they ever see the book they will understand me more. I try not to let my surroundings affect me. I work in an office but dress as I please and wear make-up. Hence, I'm considered the office freak. I don't care though; I do my job well and my boss is pleased. So he allows me the freedom to be myself. I'm fortunate in that, for I'd never wear a suit/tie for anything or anyone.

"Outside work, the way I am has an equally big impact. I only go to places where I feel part of the crowd, mainly pubs and clubs. My friends are nearly all girls. I certainly think like one and find the attitudes of most men boring or even disgusting. I just get along better with girls. Like me, they love to dress up and look good. That means bright clothes and make-up. If they were to dress in jeans and T-shirt, I probably wouldn't go out with them in the first place. Take my girlfriend, for example. She loves the way I look. If anything, the more androgynous and feminine I look and act, the more she likes me. She's wonderful and encourages me to be myself, however I want to express 'me'. Plus, she's great at dying my hair, plucking my eyebrows and doing my make-up, etc. Although I often do that myself.

"As for my old friends (before I started to wear lots of make-up and so forth),

they find me extreme and are very dissimilar to 'me'. I don't see them so much anymore. When I do, there's often an intake of breath and a look that seems to say, 'Harry is looking even freakier this time.' Followed by a mental shrug, they remember we're still friends and we do whatever we were meeting up to do. Perhaps they feel slightly apprehensive being in public with me, but I never really felt or thought about this until now. With the friends I've made more recently, well, they've always known me like this and so it's taken for granted.

"Occasionally I get surprised if someone (usually a 40-ish man or woman or even a granny) will say 'Lovely make-up' or 'It's nice to see some people still have some style.' Those rare moments are heartening and I truly wish that more people would react like that. But when ignorant kids (the most common problem) come up to me, saying 'Is that a boy or a girl?' or some other stupid line, of course it's upsetting. Can they not see, in their tracksuits and trainers, that I am a far more stunning creature in my chiffon and taffeta (pardon *Velvet Goldmine* and pardon my vanity) than they are? Obviously not, and I'm at a loss why so many of them feel the urge to express themselves in such an uncouth and ugly manner. Normally just vocal, but I've been pushed about a bit as well. Can someone explain the reasoning behind such malevolence and violence towards me? Really, the general attitude seems to be confusion, miscomprehension and fear!

"Apart from that, I've been able to avoid anything too bad. I'm not easily intimidated and would not dream of changing; kill me if I become boring and normal! I certainly act more camp when I'm all dressed up, and because of this I have met a lot of interesting and colourful people. Being like this doesn't make me a freak. I do the same most other people my age do: pubs, clubs, concerts, cinema, books, music, cooking and spending time with friends. Just the usual things really, I'm just fussier about where I'm going. I don't feel being as I am necessitates an unusual lifestyle. Other parts of my character dictate that, but that's for a different book if anyone ever asks.

"As for this book, I sincerely hope that at least it educates a few people to get a better understanding of current transgender issues. Films such as *Velvet Goldmine* and *Hedwig and the Angry Inch* certainly help, but are probably more appreciated by people who already are familiar with this scene in one form or another. The same goes for upfront androgynous musicians and singers such as *Placebo's* Brian Molko or Boy George. Actors like Jaye Davidson or Eddie Izzard are also a positive influence. Having said that, I think that some stupid people don't consider Eddie to be a real gender-bender. They probably think it's partly a stage image or whatever, which just goes to show how blind people can be. Personally I fear the world is full of too many ignorant people and educating them is next to impossible. If I had a good idea of what to do, I'd already be out there doing it..."

..WILFREEDA BEEHIVE..

"I consider myself 'the third sex', which means that I am neither man nor woman. I am 30 years old, I come from London and have felt transgendered since my childhood. Being that way has made me realize that I am very special and important to the world. I am as proud as a lion in the jungle about the way I am, and was never confused about it. Especially my friends are great and compliment me in every way; they get more of a buzz than I do. The same for my partner. I am not so sure whether this applies to my family members as well. The ones that are interested ask questions, the others don't mention it. It suits me. I certainly don't flaunt it at work, but if they ask about anything I will be honest.

"I love transforming into an exciting being and surprising the hetero world by doing so. When I go out, the woman is always in me, regardless of whether I'm clubbing, shopping or working. I would love to have breast implants and bigger lips, because it is so sexy-looking on women. I do have bits and pieces done in order to make myself look more feminine, but prefer not to go into the details. When I go out (and I go out absolutely anywhere), my friends all have similar interests. The fantastic aspect of going out is that I have met loads of straight men and straight women who all adored me like a star and wanted me!

"I also had some pretty peculiar encounters, and one stands out in particular. This happened during a trip to New York in the early Nineties, when I went to visit one of the best trannie clubs at the time, called Edelweiss. Like so many clubs, this one had a reputation for being a pick-up place, and I believe there was also a fair bit of drug-dealing going on. During the course of the evening, I was approached by this not very convincing-looking tranny and we started to talk. After showering me with affections, he then admitted that he was an undercover cop, and he only came to the club to see whether all the rumours of vice and debauchery were really true. Inevitably, he asked me in a rather probing manner, 'Do you know what's going on in here?' and, smelling a rat, I tried to look as surprised as possible. Playing Madam Innocent, I replied 'Find out for yourself, I'm just a tourist!' and this did the trick. After my convincing lie, he was relieved that I was obviously not part of all this 'debauchery' and asked me out for dinner the following week.

"One of my memorable sexual encounters was when I met a rugby player who was extremely well-built. After frolicking about and being very rampant, he wanted to feel my gold-manicured fingernails inside him! Which cost me dear because I lost four nails in the process. This excited him completely. I often chuckle to myself when I see gold nails and rugby players...

"On another memorable occcasion several years ago, I had a most thrilling encounter with the late Michael Hutchence of former Aussie band INXS. My friends and I were modelling for a Murray&Vern fashion show at the Tunnel Club in Glasgow. After the show we all went to this private party for INXS, who were touring Scotland at the time. I was in full drag and accidentally bumped into Michael, who was obviously very pleased about the collision. Although I'm not so sure whether he realized straight away that I was not a fully biological woman. It must be said that we both were not exactly sober either, and Michael certainly didn't waste any time with detours but came straight to the point. The point in question was my mouth, and it was only after my lipstick was smeared all over him and I started laughing that he must have sussed something. But this did not stop him from continuing to kiss me, and who was I to push him aside? But eventually we just laughed it off after a few more drinks and some photos, which were taken of us together.

"After this, I did get some offers from national newspapers who were interested in the photos and my story, especially because at the same time Michael was having an affair with another 'Suicide Blonde', the late Paula Yates. But then I changed my mind, because firstly I wasn't interested in doing this just for the money, and second, some things are best kept as a pleasant memory. Of course, nowadays I am at a stage where I can afford to buy my own Christian Dior – or whatever – collection. So, should any similar experience ever occur again with celebrities and photos and newspaper offers, next time around I would not sell my story either.

"In general people haven't reacted too negatively towards me, because they don't know how to handle it. I always think that the ones who are negative have perhaps more to hide than we know. Only once have I encountered abusive language, and someone spat at me like a snake. For most people it is just fear of the unknown and I'd say the general reactions are 50/50. Anyway, if the media didn't treat us like circus freaks, then dealing with the hetero world would be more tolerable. Also, it always depends on where you are - right place, right time, of course! But I am very optimistic. There is plenty I have to offer this world, and for me things will be even better than they are now."

... MR. CHARLESTON ...

"My stage name is Mr. Charleston, and I am best described as a heterosexual androgyne. I do not wish to mention my age, neither do I wish to go into details about the stage persona I have created – that's because I like to keep an element of mystery surrounding me. I currently live in Toronto, but in the past lived in London for several years. I still frequent London often, as it's the place where I feel most comfortable. When in London, it's always nice to mess with peoples minds and kick it large.

"As an androgyne, I find no real difference in attitudes, except that the Canadian culture is merely larger in size. But the personal intellect and awareness of individuals of this type are very similar.

"I felt fully androgynous by the age of fourteen, and this also shows in my features. So in that sense, my androgyny has very much a natural element to it, which I of course then take to a deeper level. However, this 'deeper level' will never include any plastic surgery or hormones, I simply wouldn't consider it.

"But I was already aware of this side at the age of eight, when people like Candy Darling and Holly Woodlawn from Warhol's Factory became familiar faces. Also, Bowie's 'Ziggy Stardust' and 'The Rocky Horror Show' influenced me considerably in terms of androgyny. It influenced my taste in music and fashion and attitude. That whole gender-bender glamrock business did it for me, I guess.

"When I go out, I go wherever I want, but I don't socialise in places of no interest to me. I roll with a crew of similar types, so I'm not the odd one out. When I'm all made up, it's not a matter of feeling excited but there is always a sense of self-awareness to it. Once I was cheered on by three drag queens; this happened when I was sixteen. A friend and I went to this boring straight club to score some dope. There, we met this bearded, really masculine-looking dealer. As it turned out shortly afterwards, he sold us bullshit dope. We hit the streets looking for him, and by luck found him in the gay district peddling his stuff. So in front of the three above-mentioned drag queens working the corner, I went exclusively for it. I proceeded to strip this motherfucker of his macho manhood and then took his real dope, his money and his knife. All to massive cheers coming from the drag queens. Mind you, I was in pearls, make-up, a purple fur coat and a black snakeskin two-piece. We don't fuck around!

"I'm always extremely fearless and proud. I'd live my days in complete loneliness and isolation if need be. 'The Loneliness Of The Long Distance Runner'. My family has never really understood me, but I don't expect them to. I moved out at fifteen, so it never was that much of a conflict anyway. I have gone to work looking very androgynous on many occasions, but being in the entertainment industry, you really don't come across conflicting attitudes. And my friends are only people who dig the way I strut. So anyone else can go screw themselves.

"The general population has, and will always have, a dislike for types like me. By that I don't only mean my attitude, but my looks too. Some people of my type unfortunately become victims to their abuse, but the truth and cause must march on regardless. It doesn't really matter whether you're fully trans-gendered, partly transgendered or androgynous – my manifesto is simple: Blood In, Blood Out. Once you're in, you're in".

I'M A GIRL

I started life 'like most' as an innocent little boy.
Running... jumping... shouting... and so full of the joy
That life endows to all... in a chromosonic way.
But somehow felt different at night... and often is the day.

Off out to play with the boys and the girls...
Just couldn't stop looking at the frocks and the curls
So soft... so gentle... so beautifully kind.
Get behind me Satan... your messing with my mind.

The feelings grew stronger as my worklife approached.
I created an image... that just could not be broached.
Tough... strong... they could not get above me.
But they could, if they wanted... just call me a 'she'.

Two decades passed by... me... engrossed in my own civil war.
Until failure crept up on me... to inform me of my flaw.
All I have owned... now suddenly gone...
Tell me oh Lord... what have I done wrong.

I now live alone as a girl... all the time.
Still tortured by the fact that I have commited a crime.
I am happy as the girl that I am... that I am.
Not beautieful... not graceful... not even glam.

So I pen my rhymes for friends like you.
Who have done so much to make all this come true.
No longer is my life in a twisted whirl.
I'm a girl... I'm a girl... I'm a girl!!!

For my transgendered sisters / Gillian Louise Andersen, 2001 glitter books THE LEADER IS INNOCENT!